high note 1

Workbook

A2/A2+

T0383558

Pearson
KAO TWO
KAO Park
Hockham Way
Harlow, Essex
CM17 9SR
England
and Associated Companies throughout the world

www.english.com/highnote

© Pearson Education Limited 2020

The right of Rod Fricker to be identified as author of this work has been asserted by him in accordance with the Copyright, Designs and Patents Act, 1988.

All rights reserved. No part of this publication may be reproduced, stored in a retrieval system, or transmitted in any form or by any means, electronic, mechanical, photocopying, recording or otherwise without the prior written permission of the Publishers.

First published 2020
Eighth impression 2024
ISBN: 978-1-292-20934-0
Set in Akko Pro
Printed by CPI Group (UK) Ltd, Croydon CRO 4YY

Image Credit(s)

The publisher would like to thank the following for their kind permisson to reproduce their photographs:

123RF.com: ahasoft2000 90, belchonock 54, captainvector 73, Christos Georghiou 73, Corey A Ford 114, Dean Drobot 83, deklofenak 10, dolgachov 97, Eric Isselee 114, ferli 23, Frantisek Chmura 118, Hongqi Zhang 13, Konstantin Pelikh 47, Konstantin Petrov 92, lightfieldstudios 19, 71, lubianova 73, macrovector 73, ostapenko 73, Patricia Hofmeester 96, Roman Babakin 16, rosipro 4, route55 73, sam74100 92, Scott Griessel 8, Sergiy Zavgorodny 107, Sorapong Chaipanya 121, Steven Coling 118, Teeramet Thanomkiat 95, Thanapol Kuptanisakorn 96, yupiramos 73; **Alamy Stock Photo**: Hemis 83, Peter Lane 78; Getty Images: apomares 107, arekmalang 95, beyhanyazar 96, Bulgac 18, Charly_Morlock 75, danchooalex 52, David Crespo 84, dolgachov 92, dusanpetkovic 77, ElenaMorgan 20, enviromantic 112, fotokon 17, Francisco Martin Gonzalez/500px 67, hadynyah 4, Hannares 117, haveseen 117, Hero Images 6, 37, Imagno 65, joakimbkk 25, londoneye 92, Maskot 80, mediaphotos 118, Michael Pavlic/EyeEm 121, miodrag ignjatovic 82, monkeybusinessimages 34, Niedring/Drentwett 27, Paul Morigi 53, peepo 89, PeopleImages 93, Perry Mastrovito 21, Peter Cade 91, Philippe Marion 46, Photography by Jeremy Villasis, Philippines 66-67, pixdeluxe 85, pixelfit 55, 94, Raylipscombe 101, Reporters Associati & Archivi 53, SDI Productions 40, 104, serts 59, 59, shironosov 29, skynesher 105, steve_is_on_holiday 113, tristan Fewings 70, Ullstein bild Dtl. 53, Vintage Images 59, Vladimir Vladimirov 9, 43, Wavebreakmedia 108, Westend61 7, Zero Creatives 28; **PA Images**: Richard Gray/EMPICS Entertainment 44, 44, 45; **Shutterstock.com**: 20th Century Fox/ Kobal 68, Aksenova Natalya 114, Anton Brand 73, ARENA Creative 118, AVIcon 90, Best3d 90, bsd 20, 20, Burana Srivakul 118, Daniel Prudek 114, Dean Drobot 103, Doctor Black 61, Edward Westmacott 114, Eric Isselee 114, Everett - Art 57, Farhads 20, Francois Poirier 90, Geanina Bechea 121, Hung Chung Chih 121, Ivan Feoktistov 21, JaumeOrpinell 58, Kamieshkova 29, Kolonko 90, Kotomiti Okuma 114, maicasaa 90, michaeljung 118, MongPro 114, Narongpon Chaibot 88, oatawa 5, Olena Yakobchuk 11, Olinchuk 33, Peryn22 82, photosync 114, PR Image Factory 31, SeamlessPatterns 107, Shift Drive 61, Somboon Bunproy 114, T-Kot 20, TopVectorElements 20, Universal/Kobal 64, WonderfulPixel 90, Yuriy Chertol 24, Zoia Kostina 13; **TheSchoolhouseLondon**: 35

Cover Image: *Front*: **Alamy Stock Photo**: Roman Lacheev

All other images © Pearson Education

Illustration acknowledgements

(Key: l-left; r-right)
Illustrated by Sean (KJA Artists) p11, p22, p32, p81, p102, p109(l); Lois (KJA Artists) p9, p41, p79; May van Millingen (Illustration Ltd) p30, p69, p103, p109(r).

Every effort has been made to trace the copyright holders and we apologise in advance for any unintentional omissions. We would be pleased to insert the appropriate acknowledgement in any subsequent edition of this publication.

CONTENTS

01 The things we do

1A GRAMMAR AND VOCABULARY

Present Simple: affirmative and negative

1 ★ Choose the correct forms to complete the sentences.

1 Alex *get* / *gets* up at 7 o'clock.
2 I *have* / *has* breakfast every day.
3 We *like* / *likes* going to school.
4 My parents *eat* / *eats* pizza on Fridays.
5 You *live* / *lives* in Scotland.
6 My teacher *give* / *gives* us homework every day.
7 Sue *come* / *comes* from Australia.
8 Max and I *play* / *plays* football on Saturdays.

2 ★ Read what Helen says and then complete the text about her with the correct forms of the Present Simple.

My name's Helen. I get up at seven o'clock on weekdays and have a shower. I get dressed and eat breakfast. I go to school at eight o'clock and have lessons from eight thirty until three o'clock. I get home at four o'clock and I do my homework. I sometimes watch television or go out with my friends.

This is Helen. She ¹*gets up* at seven o'clock on weekdays and ² _____ a shower. She ³ _____ dressed and ⁴ _____ breakfast. She ⁵ _____ to school at eight o'clock and ⁶ _____ lessons from eight thirty until three o'clock. She ⁷ _____ home at four o'clock and she ⁸ _____ her homework. She sometimes ⁹ _____ television or ¹⁰ _____ out with her friends.

3 ★ Choose the correct forms to complete the text.

Namrata and Rupa ¹ ___ in a village called Thamo in Nepal. People come here to see the beautiful mountains but for Namrata and Rupa, this is their home.

Namrata ² ___ at 6 a.m. and she ³ ___ her mother in the kitchen. They ⁴ ___ breakfast together. Rupa ⁵ ___ make breakfast. She ⁶ ___ with her father and their animals.

Namrata and Rupa ⁷ ___ to school in Namche, 5 km from their home. Sometimes they meet people from other countries on their way to school. Namrata likes to say hello, but Rupa ⁸ ___ English.

1	**a** live	**b** lives
2	**a** get up	**b** gets up
3	**a** help	**b** helps
4	**a** have	**b** has
5	**a** don't	**b** doesn't
6	**a** work	**b** works
7	**a** go	**b** goes
8	**a** speaks	**b** doesn't speak

4 ★ Find the words which don't complete the sentences correctly.

1 *She / He doesn't / They / We don't* like football.

2 *Mark / My parents / My dog / Meg* lives in England.

3 *My friends / My sister and I / My mum / Nathan and Paul* don't play chess.

4 *I / You / He / We* wear a uniform.

5 *I don't / He doesn't / We / She* come from Italy.

6 *Celine / Celine's sister / Celine and her sister / Celine's mother* speaks French.

5 ★ Use the words you chose in Exercise 4 to write correct sentences.

1 *She likes football.*

2 _____

3 _____

4 _____

5 _____

6 _____

6 ★★ Complete the sentences with the negative Present Simple forms of the verbs in brackets.

1 I like school but I *don't like* (like) homework.

2 Cherie has lunch but she _____ (have) breakfast.

3 My friends go out on weekdays but I _____ (go) out with them because I always have a lot of homework.

4 We have lessons on weekdays but we _____ (have) lessons on Saturdays.

5 My parents speak English but my dad _____ (speak) very good English.

6 My mum comes from London but she _____ (live) in London.

7 ★★ Use the prompts to write sentences in the Present Simple.

1 Emily / not have / lessons on Saturdays. She / go out / with her friends
Emily doesn't have lessons on Saturdays.

2 My mum / be from Italy / but / I / not speak / Italian
_____
_____

3 I / go to / bed / at 10 o'clock on weekdays but on Saturdays / I / not go to / bed early
_____
_____

4 My sister / wear / a uniform / at her school / but we / not wear / a uniform at our school
_____
_____

5 My parents / have breakfast / at 7 a.m. but I / not have / breakfast with them. I / get up / at 7.15
_____
_____

8 ★★★ Complete the texts with the correct Present Simple forms of the verbs from the box.

come (x2)   get up   go (x3)   have (x2)   know   like
not go   not like   not play   play

OUR ROUTINES

Javier **1***goes* shopping on Saturdays. I stay at home. I **2**_____ shopping because I **3**_____ shopping.

Klara **4**_____ to English classes on Saturday morning. She walks back home and **5**_____ lunch with her family or she **6**_____ to see me at my house and we **7**_____ lunch together.

We **8**_____ playing and watching sports. Piotr **9**_____ football for the school team. I **10**_____ football but I watch football.

My brother **11**_____ very early on Saturdays because he **12**_____ to work at 7 a.m. He **13**_____ into my room and says: 'Good morning!'. He **14**_____ that I want to sleep!

9 ★★★ Use the information to complete the sentences in the Present Simple.

	Mark	Susie	Michelle
get up	7 a.m.	7.30 a.m.	7.30 a.m.
have a shower	✗	✓	✓
wear a uniform	✓	✗	✗
speak English	✓	✓	✗
Saturday	go to a Spanish class	go shopping	go shopping

1 Mark *gets up* at 7 a.m. Susie and Michelle _____ at 7.30 a.m.

2 Mark _____ a shower in the morning. Susie and Michelle _____ a shower every morning.

3 At school, Mark _____ a uniform. Susie and Michelle _____ a uniform.

4 Mark and Susie _____ but Michelle_____ English.

5 On Saturday, Mark _____ and Susie and Michelle _____.

10 ON A HIGH NOTE Write five true sentences about your own daily routine using five different verbs from the lesson. Make at least two negative sentences.

1B VOCABULARY | Free-time activities and frequency expressions

1 ★ **Choose two correct words to complete the sentences.**

1 Maxine goes *shopping / sport / to the cinema* on Saturdays.
2 Francine doesn't play *sport / computer games / lessons*.
3 I go to *the cinema / shopping / a friend's house* after school on Fridays.
4 I watch *TV / parties / films* with my friends.
5 My parents listen to *books / music / the radio* in the evening.

2 ★★ **Complete the sentences with one word in each gap.**

1 Lesley g*oes* shopping after school.
2 Sven h_____ o_____ with his friends in the shopping centre on Saturdays.
3 Selena g_____ t_____ her friend's house on Sundays.
4 Janice p_____ games on her mobile phone on the bus to school.
5 Paula l_____ t_____ music in her room.
6 Simon r_____ books – he loves books.
7 Ela and Justina w_____ films on television.
8 Cass w_____ a blog about her cat.

3 ★★ **Complete the text with the words from the box.**

~~cinema~~ football homework lessons party school shopping sport

I do a lot in my free time. I go to the **¹***cinema* to watch films. Once a week, I play **²**_____. I play **³**_____ and tennis. Once a month I go to a **⁴**_____ at a friend's house and once a week I go **⁵**_____ with my parents or my friends. I have Spanish **⁶**_____ twice a week on Mondays and Thursdays. I go to **⁷**_____ five days a week and I do **⁸**_____ six days a week – but that isn't free time!

4 ★ **Match sentences 1–6 with frequency expressions a–f.**

1 ☐ I have French lessons on Tuesdays and Fridays.
2 ☐ I eat breakfast, lunch and dinner.
3 ☐ We have exams in January and June.
4 ☐ My parents go for a meal every June 15th.
5 ☐ My sister has a shower in the morning and in the evening.
6 ☐ I hang out with friends every Saturday.

a once a year
b once a week
c twice a week
d twice a day
e twice a year
f three times a day

5 ★★ **Look at Debbie's calendar and complete the sentences with the correct frequency expressions.**

1 She goes to school *five times a week*.
2 She goes to a dance class _____.
3 She tidies her room _____.
4 She visits her grandma _____.
5 She goes to the cinema _____.
6 She goes to an art club _____.

OCTOBER					
Mon	30 (Sept) art club	7 art club	14 art club	21 art club	28 art club
Tues	1 art club	8 art club	15 art club	22 art club	29 art club
Wed	2 dance class	9 dance class	16 dance class	23 dance class	30 dance class
Thurs	3 art club	10 art club	17 art club	24 art club	31 art club
Fri	4 dance class	11 dance class	18 dance class	25 dance class	1 (Nov) dance class
Sat	5 no school cinema tidy room	12 no school tidy room	19 no school tidy room	26 no school tidy room	2 (Nov) no school cinema tidy room
Sun	6 no school	13 no school visit grandma	20 no school	27 no school visit grandma	3 (Nov) no school

6 ON A HIGH NOTE **Describe what you do in your free time. Write when you do it and how often you do it.**

UNIT VOCABULARY PRACTICE > page 13

1C GRAMMAR

Adverbs of frequency

1 ★ Put the adverbs of frequency from the box in the correct order.

hardly ever   never   often   sometimes   ~~usually~~

1 _____   2 _____   3 _____   4 _____   5 _usually_   always

2 ★★ Rewrite the sentences with the adverbs of frequency in brackets in the correct place.

1 I am tired at school. (sometimes)
I am sometimes tired at school.

2 I eat chips. (hardly ever)
_____

3 My mum works late. (often)
_____

4 My dad is angry. (never)
_____

5 This shop has some great things to buy. (usually)
_____

6 My friend checks her phone when I'm with her. (always)
_____

3 ★★★ Replace the underlined phrases with the adverbs of frequency from Exercise 1. Use each adverb once. You may need to change the word order of the sentences.

1 I go to the cinema about once a year.
I hardly ever go to the cinema.

2 I don't eat meat. I don't like it.
_____

3 Sam goes to school by bus every day.
_____

4 My parents are at home in the evenings nearly every day.
_____

5 Once or twice a month our teacher gives us a test.
_____

6 Abigail is late for school three times a week.
_____

Present Simple: questions

4 ★ Match questions 1–5 with short answers a–e.

1 ☐ Does your sister wear a uniform?
2 ☐ Do your parents play sport?
3 ☐ Does Mr Smith work in London?
4 ☐ Do you and your friends often go shopping?
5 ☐ Do you get up late on Sundays?

a Yes, he does.
b No, they don't.
c Yes, we do.
d No, I don't.
e No, she doesn't.

5 ★★ Read the questions and write positive and negative short answers.

1 Does your mum play computer games?
Yes, she does. / _____

2 Do your friends write blogs?
_____ / _____

3 Do you often go shopping?
_____ / _____

4 Does your dad work at the weekend?
_____ / _____

5 Do you and your friends go out on weekdays?
_____ / _____

6 ★★★ Read the answers and complete the questions.

1 _How often do you_ go shopping?
I go shopping about twice a week.

2 Where _____ work?
My dad works in Manchester.

3 What time _____ go to bed?
My parents go to bed at about 11 p.m.

4 How _____ go to school?
I go to school by bus.

5 What _____ do in the evenings?
My sister watches TV and chats to her friends.

6 Who _____ usually talk to on the phone?
I usually talk to my friend Sara.

7 ON A HIGH NOTE Answer the questions in Exercise 6 so they are true for you.

1D READING AND VOCABULARY

1 Read comments 1–5 quickly and write the names of the people in the pictures.

A *Abdul*

B _____

C _____

D _____

E _____

2 Read the comments again and choose the correct answers.

1 Camilla says that
   a she isn't surprised that her parents are upset.
   b her parents are right about her.
   c her friends have the same problem.

2 When Abdul meets people
   a he never talks to them.
   b he tries to find out things about them.
   c he talks about himself.

3 Meghan says that
   a she doesn't need much sleep at night.
   b she decides when she goes to bed, not her parents.
   c her parents don't believe she doesn't chat to friends at night.

4 We know that
   a Conrad's mum works at the weekend.
   b Conrad doesn't like going out.
   c Conrad helps his mum at home.

5 Which sentence is true about Leila's brother?
   a He doesn't have any free time on weekdays.
   b He doesn't go out at the weekend.
   c He doesn't do any work in the evenings.

Vocabulary extension

3 Choose the correct meanings for the underlined words from the text.

1 Max <u>cares about</u> his school work.
   It *is / isn't* important for him.

2 Tom <u>feels upset</u> when his parents are angry.
   He doesn't *like / mind* it.

3 I <u>stay up late</u> on Fridays.
   I *go to bed late in the evening / get up late in the morning*.

4 Luther is very <u>lazy</u>.
   He *works / doesn't work* hard.

5 Donna is a <u>talkative</u> girl.
   She *likes / doesn't like* talking very much.

4 Complete the sentences with the correct forms of the underlined words from Exercise 3.

1 Why is Paul so <u>*talkative*</u> today? He's usually quiet.

2 I'm not _____. I always work hard.

3 I _____ when my friends don't talk to me.

4 I _____ my little brother but I don't like staying at home to look after him when one of my friends has a party.

5 I can't believe that you sometimes _____ on a school day!

ACTIVE VOCABULARY | Antonyms

It is a good idea to learn some words with their antonyms. It is easier to learn more words when you learn them in pairs. These can be:
- adjectives (e.g. *good – bad*)
- adverbs (e.g. *always – never*)
- verbs (e.g. *start – finish*)

5 Match words 1–7 from the text with their antonyms a–g.

1 ☐ shy   **a** find
2 ☐ new   **b** answer
3 ☐ lose   **c** remember
4 ☐ true   **d** confident
5 ☐ forget   **e** early
6 ☐ late   **f** old
7 ☐ ask   **g** false

6 Complete the sentences with the correct words from Exercise 5.

1 I like meeting new people but I'm quite <u>*shy*</u> and I never know what to say.

2 Hurry! I don't want to be _____ for school.

3 I get nervous when our teachers _____ me questions.

4 This is a(n) _____ house. Here's a photo of the house from 1895.

5 It really happened. It's a _____ story.

6 Where's my pen? I can't _____ it.

7 Do you _____ your first day at school?

7 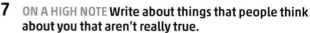 ON A HIGH NOTE Write about things that people think about you that aren't really true.

People
HAVE THE WRONG IDEA
about me

1 Camilla

My parents often tell me that I don't understand money. I know why they're upset. I often lose things, but it isn't because I don't care about them. My problem is that I put something down on the table and then forget it. When I realise, I feel very upset, but I don't know how to change it. My friends can't help me because it never happens to them.

2 Abdul

I'm quite shy and I don't like talking about myself, so when I meet new people, I ask them lots of questions. People who are talkative don't know I'm quiet. I don't have time to say anything! And they think I'm confident!

3 Meghan

A lot of my friends stay up late in the evening and chat on social media. I always go to bed at 10.30 so I can't chat with them. My friends think that I don't chat because of my parents. When I tell them it's my choice and that I like going to bed early because I need a lot of sleep, they don't believe me!

4 Conrad

I stay in a lot. My friends think that I don't like going out, but it isn't true. I live with my mum and my little sister. My mum works in the evenings so, when I get home, I cook dinner and help my sister. At the weekend, I do housework. I just haven't got time to go out.

5 Leila

My brother says I'm lazy because I always have a lot of free time during the school week. It isn't true, I just get things done quickly. My brother can only go out with his friends on Friday evenings and Saturdays because he sits at his desk from 4 p.m. to 11 p.m. but still doesn't finish his homework. Why not? Because he spends a lot of time looking at his phone and writing to friends.

1E SPEAKING

1 🔊 *2* Listen and repeat the phrases. How do you say them in your language?

SPEAKING | Talking about likes and dislikes

ASKING ABOUT LIKES AND DISLIKES

What's your favourite film?

What kind of books **does he like reading**?

Does he **enjoy reading** fantasy books?

LIKE/ENJOY/LOVE

You **like reading** fantasy books (a lot).

He **enjoys playing** computer games.

He **loves going** to the cinema.

QUITE LIKE/DON'T MIND

I **quite like watching** films at the cinema.

I **don't mind staying** in on Saturdays.

DON'T LIKE/CAN'T STAND/HATE

I **don't like staying** in on Saturdays.

I **can't stand playing** computer games.

I **hate doing** exercise.

2 Complete the sentences with the correct forms of the verbs in brackets.

1 Do you enjoy *playing* (play) computer games?
2 My dad loves _____ (watch) old films.
3 My mum likes _____ (go) shopping on Saturdays.
4 I hate _____ (read) old books.
5 My sister can't stand _____ (get) up early.
6 Do your parents like _____ (go) for walks?

3 Complete the sentences with one word in each gap.

1 Some of my friends can't s*tand* playing sport.
2 What k_____ of music do you like?
3 I q_____ like reading but I prefer using my computer.
4 I don't m_____ going to school – I meet my friends there.
5 What's your f_____ sport?
6 Do you e_____ shopping with your parents?

4 Choose the correct responses to complete the mini-conversations.

1

Heather Do you want to go shopping tomorrow?

Chris No, thanks. ___ shopping.

a I don't mind   **b** I enjoy   **c** I hate

2

Lola Do you enjoy going out on Saturdays?

Bella Yes, but ___ staying in. I can read or play computer games.

a I can't stand   **b** I don't mind   **c** I don't like

3

Sally What kind of books do you like reading?

Jackie ___ books about real people's lives.

a My favourite   **b** I enjoy   **c** My kind of

4

Mia ___ playing football.

Rory Why? Football's OK.

Mia No, it isn't.

a I can't stand   **b** I don't mind   **c** I quite like

5

Tim Do you like watching fantasy films?

Hannah I quite enjoy them but ___.

a I prefer action films

b they're my favourite

c I can't stand them

5 Complete the dialogues with the correct forms of the words from the box.

go   kind   mind   ~~play~~   read   sit   spend   stand

Alison Do you like ¹*playing* sport?

Conor Not really. I don't ²_____ watching sports on TV but I love ³_____ – books, newspapers, magazines. My favourite ⁴_____ of books are fantasy books.

Sandra Do you enjoy ⁵_____ to the cinema?

Alex No, I don't. I hate ⁶_____ next to someone with a mobile phone and I can't ⁷_____ people eating popcorn near me. Also, I don't like ⁸_____ money!

1F LISTENING AND VOCABULARY

1 🔊 *3* **Listen and match speakers 1–3 with hobbies a–e. There are two extra hobbies.**

1 ☐ Tom
2 ☐ Annie
3 ☐ Alex

a creating something
b collecting things
c playing a game
d travelling to different places
e learning something new

2 🔊 *3* **Listen again and choose the correct answers.**

1 Which page does Tom show to Alina?

2 Where does Annie practise?

3 Where can you hear Alex's tunes?

Vocabulary extension

3 🔊 *4* **Complete the extracts from the recording in Exercise 1 with the words from the box. Listen and check.**

around   down   in   ~~into~~   on   so

1 I organise them *into* groups.
2 I listen online, repeat the words four or five times and then write them _____ .
3 I don't write _____ Chinese!
4 I dream about travelling _____ the world.
5 I know 63 words _____ far.
6 People can listen to the music and comment _____ it.

4 **ON A HIGH NOTE Write about one or more of your hobbies.**

Pronunciation

> ### ACTIVE PRONUNCIATION | The final s in plural nouns
>
> Plural nouns end in s which we pronounce in three different ways:
> - /s/ (e.g. book**s**, pet**s**)
> - /z/ (e.g. gam**es**, boy**s**)
> - /ɪz/ (e.g. box**es**, house**s**)

5 🔊 *5* **Look at three ways of pronouncing the letter s at the end of a plural word. Listen and repeat the three sounds.**

/s/   /z/   /ɪz/

6 🔊 *6* **Listen and repeat these three words from the recording in Exercise 1. Match them with the three sounds from Exercise 5.**

pla**ces** _____
spor**ts** _____
frien**ds** _____

7 🔊 *7* **Listen to ten more plural words from the recording in Exercise 1 and write them in the correct column.**

James has some interesting thing**s**.

/s/	/z/	/ɪz/
	museums	

8 🔊 *8* **Practise saying these sentences. Listen and repeat.**

1 I like dog**s**, cat**s**, computer**s** and book**s**.
2 I've got two brother**s**, two sister**s**, two parent**s** and lots of friend**s**.
3 In my bag, there are headphone**s**, sunglass**es**, pen**s** and key**s**.
4 At the meeting there were scientist**s**, nurs**es**, actor**s** and vet**s**.
5 After school you can go to club**s**, play sport**s**, do extra lesson**s** and other thing**s**.

UNIT VOCABULARY PRACTICE > page 13

1G WRITING | A personal profile

> Introduce yourself: name, age, country, nationality, family.

> Talk about your daily life: school, clubs.

> Talk about your free time: likes and dislikes.

I'm Darsha. I'm 16 and I'm ¹*from* the UK. I live with my parents, two brothers and one sister in West London. My grandparents ²l_____ in Delhi, India so I don't see them often.

On schooldays I ³g_____ up at 7 a.m. I usually get home at 4 p.m. but twice a ⁴w_____ I play basketball so I don't get home until 5 p.m. I also go to music school to learn the piano, but I don't like it because it's very difficult.

I ⁵e_____ spending time with my family. My mum teaches me to cook Indian food. I enjoy cooking and the food is delicious. My sister and I ⁶o_____ go shopping for clothes together. There are some great clothes shops near our house. I also like reading and watching films. My ⁷f_____ film is *Monsoon Wedding*.

1 Read the profile and complete the notes.

Name:	¹*Darsha*
Brother(s):	² _____
Sister(s):	³ _____
Grandparents live in:	⁴ _____
Sports:	⁵ _____
Extra lessons:	⁶ _____
Interests:	cooking, shopping,
	⁷ _____ ,
	⁸ _____

2 Complete the profile with one word in each gap.

3 Where could sentences 1–4 go in the profile? Write the first three words of the sentences from the profile after which you could use sentences 1–4.

1 *My grandparents live* ... . We visit them once a year.
2 _____ ... . I have breakfast and walk to school with my friends.
3 _____ ... . We sometimes go after school, but we usually go on Saturdays when we have more time.
4 _____ ... . It's very funny.

4 Complete the sentences from the profile with *and*, *but*, *so* and *because*. Then look at the profile and check your answers.

1 I live with my parents, two brothers *and* one sister in West London.
2 My grandparents live in Delhi, India _____ I don't see them often.
3 I usually get home at 4 p.m. _____ twice a week I play basketball so I don't get home until 5 p.m.
4 I also go to music school to learn the piano, _____ I don't like it _____ it's very difficult.
5 I also like reading _____ watching films.

5 Complete the sentences with *and*, *but*, *so* and *because*.

1 I sometimes write a blog, *but* I don't write every day.
2 I go walking every day _____ we've got a dog.
3 My friends live near me _____ I see them a lot.
4 I play basketball _____ football.
5 We sometimes go to India _____ my grandparents live there.
6 I don't like films _____ I don't go to the cinema.

6 WRITING TASK Think of a friend or family member that you know very well. Use the information below and your imagination to write their profile.

ACTIVE WRITING | A personal profile

1 Plan your profile.
- Think of some facts about their age, nationality and family.
- Make notes about their daily routine. Ask them for details if you aren't sure.
- Make brief notes about their interests, likes and dislikes.

2 Write the profile.
- Use three paragraphs to organise your profile.
- Use the Present Simple and adverbs of frequency to talk about daily routine.
- Use *like/enjoy/hate + -ing* to talk about likes and dislikes.
- Use *and*, *but*, *because* and *so*.

3 Check that ...
- you have included all the relevant information.
- there are no spelling or grammar mistakes.
- you have used relevant topic vocabulary.

1 1A GRAMMAR AND VOCABULARY **Complete the sentences with a preposition in each gap.**

1 I have Spanish lessons _on_ Mondays _____ the afternoon.

2 Tom has a shower _____ the morning and _____ the evening.

3 My parents go to bed _____ 11 o'clock _____ night.

4 Katie's birthday is _____ March.

5 I don't study _____ Saturdays, but I do homework _____ Sunday mornings.

6 _____ weekdays I go to bed _____ 10 o'clock but _____ the weekend I go to bed _____ midnight.

2 1A GRAMMAR AND VOCABULARY **Choose the correct words to complete the sentences.**

1 I don't _do / have / get_ exercises in the morning.

2 Some people _have / get / go_ to school on Saturdays.

3 Melanie _does / gets / goes_ dressed in her bedroom.

4 My dad _does / goes / has_ his lunch at work.

5 I _do / have / go_ a shower in the morning.

6 Ellie _goes / has / gets_ shopping on Saturdays.

7 I don't _get / go / do_ up at 7 o'clock in the morning.

8 My sister and I _get / do / go_ homework in the evening.

3 1B VOCABULARY **Complete the texts with the words from the box.**

go   go to   hang   listen   ~~play~~   read   watch   write

4 1D READING AND VOCABULARY **Match the two parts of the questions and complete them with one word in each gap.**

1 ☐ What time do you get

2 ☐ How often do you stay

3 ☐ Why don't you look

4 ☐ Why do you always put your phone

5 ☐ Do you want to put

a _____ some music?

b _____ on the table?

c _____ home from school?

d it _____ on the Internet?

e _____ on Saturday evenings and how often do you go out?

5 1F LISTENING AND VOCABULARY **Complete the sentences with the correct verbs.**

1 Don't be nervous about speaking French. People don't l<u>augh</u> at you just because you make a few mistakes when you try to speak their language.

2 Do you want to t_____ me about your holiday?

3 I don't a_____ with you about music but I like the films you watch.

4 My friends don't like w_____ for me when I'm late.

5 Matt often d_____ about life when he's 25 and has got lots of money.

6 ON A HIGH NOTE **Write about things you like doing, can't stand doing and don't mind doing.**

MY FREE TIME

COMMENTS

Nice blog! My friends and I like the same things. We ¹_play_ computer games, we ²_____ films, we ³_____ parties and we ⁴_____ to music.

Sean, 16

I ⁵_____ out with my friends at the weekend. We usually ⁶_____ shopping.
I stay at home in the evening. I ⁷_____ a blog and I ⁸_____ books.

Hazel, 15

1 **For each learning objective, write 1–5 to assess your ability.**

1 = I don't feel confident. 5 = I feel confident.

	Learning objective	Course material	How confident I am (1–5)
1A	I can use the Present Simple to talk about daily routines.	Student's Book pp. 12–13 Workbook pp. 4–5	
1B	I can talk about free-time activities and hobbies.	Student's Book p. 14 Workbook p. 6	
1C	I can ask and answer questions about everyday life and use adverbs of frequency.	Student's Book p. 15 Workbook p. 7	
1D	I can understand the main idea of a paragraph and talk about stereotypes.	Student's Book pp. 16–17 Workbook pp. 8–9	
1E	I can talk about likes and dislikes.	Student's Book p. 18 Workbook p. 10	
1F	I can understand a simple personal podcast and talk about guilty pleasures.	Student's Book p. 19 Workbook p. 11	
1G	I can write a personal profile.	Student's Book p. 20 Workbook p. 12	

2 **Which of the skills above would you like to improve in? How?**

Skill I want to improve in	How I can improve

3 **What can you remember from this unit?**

New words I learned and most want to remember	Expressions and phrases I liked	English I heard or read outside class

GRAMMAR AND VOCABULARY

1 Choose the correct words to complete the text.

This is my normal weekend. It starts **1**___ Friday evenings. I **2**___ do homework – Friday is a time to relax, not work. I **3**___ home from school **4**___ about four o'clock. After dinner, I go out and meet my friends. Sometimes we go to a café, sometimes we go to the cinema and about once **5**___ month we go to a party.

1 a on	**b** at	**c** in
2 a sometimes	**b** usually	**c** never
3 a go to	**b** get	**c** take
4 a in	**b** on	**c** at
5 a in	**b** a	**c** for

/ 5

2 Use one word to complete both sentences.

1
a What do you do _at_ the weekend?
b Don't laugh _at_ me! Children's cartoons are my guilty pleasure.

2
a It's quiet in here. We can _____ some music on.
b I _____ my bag down on the floor and now I can't find it.

3
a I want to stay _____ tonight. I'm tired.
b My birthday is _____ January, on the 23rd.

4
a I often dream _____ being a TV or film star.
b Tell me _____ Meg's party and show me the photos!

5
a What time do you get _____ at the weekend?
b You can look _____ the word in a dictionary.

6
a I always _____ a shower in the morning.
b What time do you _____ breakfast on schooldays?

/ 5

3 Put the words in order to make sentences.

1 after / play / school / friends / chess / my / never
My friends never play chess after school.

2 late / your / often / for / lessons / you / are / ?
_____

3 reality / often / TV / watch / don't / I
_____

4 to / of / like / music / all / I / kinds / listening
_____

5 is / of / think / watching / time / a / I / waste / television
_____

6 week / lessons / have / a / twice / guitar / I
_____

/ 5

4 Use the words in brackets to complete the sentences in the Present Simple.

1 _Do you wear_ (you/wear) a uniform at your school?
2 My dad _____ (often/sing) in the shower.
3 _____ (your mum/like) listening to music?
4 My sister _____ (not read) books but she loves celebrity magazines.
5 How often _____ (Ellie/check) her mobile phone?
6 Our parties _____ (always/be) amazing.

/ 5

USE OF ENGLISH

5 Complete the conversation with one word in each gap.

Jasper Hi. Can I ask you some questions?
Millie Of course.
Jasper How often do you **1**_do_ exercise?
Millie Exercise? Never! Oh, wait. Sometimes I dance in **2**_____ of the mirror!
Jasper **3**_____ your mum send you messages when you are out with your friends?
Millie No, she doesn't. Well, only when I'm late.
Jasper Do you **4**_____ extra lessons at the weekend?
Millie No! I go out with my friends at the weekend. I have extra lessons on weekdays. I go to dance lessons twice a **5**_____ – on Mondays and Wednesdays. And I have French lessons three **6**_____ a week, on Tuesdays, Wednesdays and Thursdays.

/ 5

6 Complete the second sentence using the word in bold so that it means the same as the first one. Use no more than three words including the word in bold.

1 I meet my friends and come home late. **UNTIL**
I meet my friends and stay _out until_ late.

2 I think you are right. **WITH**
I _____ you.

3 I often visit my grandparents on Saturday or Sunday. **WEEKEND**
I often visit my grandparents _____.

4 I hate our school uniform. **STAND**
I _____ our school uniform.

5 Is your home in London? **LIVE**
Do _____ London?

6 I only write emails once or twice a year. **EVER**
I _____ emails.

/ 5
/ 30

02 No place like home

2A GRAMMAR AND VOCABULARY

There is/There are with some and any

Part 1

FLAT FOR SALE

- 2 bedrooms
- 1 bathroom
- Big living room
- Big kitchen with table (no dining room)
- Balcony (no terrace)
- Attic (no cellar)
- New windows
- No stairs!

1 ★ Read Part 1 of the advert and complete the sentences with *there is*, *there isn't*, *there are* or *there aren't*.

1 *There are* two bedrooms.
2 _____ one bathroom.
3 _____ a big living room.
4 _____ new windows.
5 _____ a balcony but _____ a terrace.
6 _____ an attic but _____ a cellar.
7 _____ a big kitchen but _____ a dining room.
8 _____ any stairs.

2 ★ Read Part 1 of the advert again and match questions 1–8 with answers a–d. Each answer matches two questions.

1 ☐ Are there two bedrooms?
2 ☐ Is there a balcony?
3 ☐ Is there a cellar?
4 ☐ Are there any stairs?
5 ☐ Is there a dining room?
6 ☐ Are there new windows?
7 ☐ Is there an attic?
8 ☐ Are there two bathrooms?

a Yes, there are.
b No, there isn't.
c Yes, there is.
d No, there aren't.

Part 2

- No study but lots of room for a desk and working area in the living room
- White walls in all rooms
- Windows in the attic
- Garage for two cars
- Trees outside
- Lovely park near the flat

3 ★ Read Part 2 of the advert in Exercise 1 and answer the questions.

1 Is there a garage? *Yes, there is.*
2 Are there any trees outside? _____
3 Are there any windows in the attic? _____
4 Is there a park near the flat? _____
5 Are there any yellow walls? _____
6 Is there a study? _____

4 ★ You still want to know more about the flat in Exercise 1. Complete the questions with the correct forms of *there is* and *there are*.

1 *Is there* wi-fi in the flat?
2 _____ a big hall in the flat?
3 _____ any children in the other flats?
4 _____ a place for bikes?
5 _____ any shops in the area?
6 _____ a school near the flat?

16

5 ⭐⭐ **Complete the dialogue with the correct forms of *there is* and *there are*.**

Magda Hi, Dana. I've found a perfect flat near the university. It's cheap and it has two floors.

Dana Two floors? So, **¹***are there* stairs in the flat?

Magda Yes. Upstairs, **²**_____ two bedrooms.

Dana **³**_____ a bathroom upstairs?

Magda Yes, **⁴**_____. And **⁵**_____ a bathroom downstairs, too.

Dana Great! **⁶**_____ a dining room?

Magda No, **⁷**_____ but **⁸**_____ a study.

Dana A study! That's good. **⁹**_____ a terrace?

Magda Yes, and **¹⁰**_____ two balconies.

Dana And is it really cheap? What's wrong with it?

Magda Well, let's go and find out!

6 ⭐⭐ **Complete the sentences with *a*, *some* or *any*.**

1 Is there *a* bathroom upstairs?

2 Are there _____ people here?

3 There are _____ big speakers in the living room.

4 Look. There's _____ guitar on the balcony.

5 There are _____ books for you in the living room.

6 There aren't _____ lessons today.

7 ⭐⭐ **USE OF ENGLISH Choose the correct words a–c to complete the text.**

Hi Saul,

We're on holiday in Spain. We've got a great 'casa', that's a house. **¹**__ some awesome pictures inside the house. There are also **²**__ Spanish film posters. I think the people who live here are artists or musicians. There is **³**__ piano in the living room too.

The balcony is very big! There's **⁴**__ table and we have breakfast outside in the morning.

You know a lot about music. Are there **⁵**__ good Spanish singers or bands?

There's **⁶**__ fiesta (party) tonight. I love parties!

See you soon,

Daniel

1 a Is there	**b** There are	**c** There is
2 a any	**b** a	**c** some
3 a some	**b** any	**c** a
4 a a	**b** some	**c** any
5 a some	**b** any	**c** a
6 a some	**b** any	**c** a

8 ⭐⭐ **Put the words in order to make sentences.**

1 is / studio / there / in / town / music / this / a / ?
Is there a music studio in this town?

2 in / some / the / are / bedroom / musical / there / instruments
_____

3 the / a / there / on / wall / poster / is
_____

4 isn't / there / bedroom / computer / in / a / my
_____

5 there / big / house / a / is / garden / behind / the / ?
_____

6 any / weekend / are / this / there / parties / ?
_____

9 ⭐⭐⭐ **USE OF ENGLISH Complete the dialogue with one word in each gap.**

Amelia Hi, Tom. It's Amelia. Where are you?

Tom Hi, Amelia. I'm in a place called Szymbark in Poland. There **¹***is* a famous house here. There **²**_____ a lot of people here to see it.

Amelia Why is it famous?

Tom Well, it's a normal house – there's **³**_____ roof and there are some windows. There are some stairs inside the house, but the house is upside down! The ceiling is down, and the floor is up. I'm inside now. When I look up, **⁴**_____ are chairs and tables above me. It's very strange. Wait a minute …

Amelia Hello?

Tom It's OK. I'm outside again now. There are **⁵**_____ other things to see here but it's time for lunch. There aren't **⁶**_____ burger bars but there are **⁷**_____ restaurants with traditional Polish food. Wait a minute. There **⁸**_____ some English people here. I can ask them about the food. Speak to you later.

Amelia OK. Enjoy your lunch. Bye.

10 ON A HIGH NOTE **Write a description of a friend's house.**

2B VOCABULARY | Rooms and furniture

1 ★ Complete the words with one letter in each gap.

Bedroom
1 w a r d r o b e
2 s _ _ _ _ f
3 b _ _ _

Kitchen
4 c _ _ _ k _ _ _
5 f _ _ d _ _ _
6 d _ _ h _ _ s _ _ r

Bathroom
7 s h _ w _ _ _
8 m _ r _ _ _ r
9 w _ _ h _ _ s _ n

Living room
10 a _ _ _ c _ _ _ _ r
11 f _ _ _ _ p _ _ _ c _
12 c _ _ _ p _ t

2 ★★ Match the words from Exercise 1 with the definitions.

1 You keep clothes in it. _wardrobe_
2 You put it on the floor to make it look nice. _____
3 You wash hands in it. It's in the bathroom. _____
4 It's a comfortable thing to sit on, but you can't lie on it. _____
5 You can wash your whole body in this. _____
6 It's a machine to clean cups and plates in. _____
7 You use it to cook food. _____

3 ★★ Complete the text with the words from the box.

armchair ~~bar~~ fireplace mirror shelf shower sofa TV wardrobe

I like our house. There isn't a dining room but there's a big kitchen with a breakfast ¹_bar_ where we can sit and eat. In the living room we've got a big, comfortable ²_____ for three people and a comfortable ³_____ – that's my dad's. There's a lovely warm ⁴_____ when it's cold. I love sitting in front of it on a winter night watching ⁵_____.

Every bedroom has a bathroom so I don't mind when my dad is in the ⁶_____ for twenty minutes in the morning or my sister wants to look at her face in the ⁷_____.

In my bedroom, there's a desk and a ⁸_____. I keep my books and CDs on it. I've got a big ⁹_____ for my clothes but there are always some clothes on the floor!

4 ★★ Look at the photo above and decide if the sentences are true or false. Rewrite the false sentences to make them true.

1 ☒ F There is a wardrobe opposite the desk.
There is a wardrobe next to the desk.
2 ☐ There is a small lamp between the wardrobe and the bed.
_____
3 ☐ There is a chair behind the desk.
_____
4 ☐ The bed is next to the wall.
_____
5 ☐ There is a laptop on the desk.
_____
6 ☐ There are some flowers under the desk.
_____

5 ★★★ USE OF ENGLISH Choose the correct words a–c to complete the text.

My kitchen

Let me tell you about our kitchen. There are lots of ¹__ with things in them. There's a big ²__ to keep food cold. There is also a shelf. ³__ the shelf, there are books about cooking and a radio. My mum likes listening to music in the kitchen. ⁴__ to the radio there is a photo of our family.

We haven't got a dishwasher. We do the washing up in the ⁵__. We haven't got a microwave, either so we do all our cooking in the cooker. The cooker is ⁶__ the fridge and the sink. Opposite the cooker there is a table. That's where we eat. Our dog is usually ⁷__ the table. He sleeps on a ⁸__ there.

1 a wardrobes	**b** cupboards	**c** carpets
2 a cooker	**b** fridge	**c** microwave
3 a On	**b** In	**c** Between
4 a Opposite	**b** In front	**c** Next
5 a washbasin	**b** sink	**c** washing machine
6 a next	**b** in front	**c** between
7 a on	**b** under	**c** in
8 a rug	**b** shelf	**c** shower

6 ON A HIGH NOTE Write about a room in your house. Say what there is in the room and where it is.

UNIT VOCABULARY PRACTICE > page 25

2C GRAMMAR AND VOCABULARY

Can/can't

1 ⭐ **Look at the notes and complete the sentences with *can* or *can't* and the correct verb.**

	Alison	Harry
cook dinner	✓	✓
iron clothes	✗	✗
speak French	✓	✗
play the guitar	✓	✗
play the piano	✓	✓
speak Spanish	✗	✓

1 Alison *can cook* dinner.
2 She _____ French but she _____ Spanish.
3 She _____ the piano and she _____ the guitar.
4 Harry _____ dinner but he _____ clothes.
5 He _____ the guitar but he _____ the piano.
6 Alison and Harry _____ dinner but they _____ clothes.

2 ⭐ **Use the information in Exercise 1 to match questions 1–6 with answers a–f.**

1 ☐ Can Alison cook dinner?
2 ☐ Can Alison speak Spanish?
3 ☐ Can Alison and Harry iron clothes?
4 ☐ Can Alison and Harry play the piano?
5 ☐ Can Harry iron clothes?
6 ☐ Can Harry cook dinner?

a Yes, they can.
b No, they can't.
c No, he can't.
d Yes, she can.
e Yes, he can.
f No, she can't.

3 ⭐⭐ **Read the questions and write short answers.**

1 Can Paul's dad drive?
✓ *Yes, he can.*
2 Can your mum cook Italian food?
✓ _____
3 Can you read books in Russian?
✗ _____
4 Can you ride a bike?
✓ _____
5 Can you and your friends play tennis?
✓ _____
6 Can your friends play musical instruments?
✗ _____

4 ⭐⭐ **Put the words in order to make sentences.**

1 you / Turkish / can / speak / ?
Can you speak Turkish?
2 dad / online / your / information / look / up / can / ?
_____
3 can't / mum / friends / always / my / my / understand
_____
4 can / school / I / from / my / house / my / see
_____
5 roof / dad / your / your / on / climb / can / ?
_____
6 pictures / friend / good / my / very / best / paint / can
_____

5 ⭐⭐⭐ **Use the prompts to write questions and answers using *can*.**

1 your brother / use / the washing machine? ✗
Can your brother use the washing machine?
No, he can't.
2 you and your sister / make / a cup of tea? ✓
_____
_____
3 your dad / cook dinner? ✓ eggs but ✗ meat
_____
_____
4 you / do / the washing up? ✓ but / not enjoy it!
_____
_____
5 your friends / drive? ✗
_____
_____
6 your parents / dance? ✓ mum but ✗ dad
_____
_____

6 ON A HIGH NOTE **Write about things you can and can't do. Write which of the things you can do you like doing and which you don't like doing.**

2D READING AND VOCABULARY

1 Look at the photos under the text and guess the answers to the questions.

  1 Whose house do you think this is?

    a grandparents' house

    b school friend's house

  2 Which words do you expect the writer to use?

    a modern, exciting, cool

    b warm, comfortable, lovely

2 Read the text quickly and check the answers to the questions in Exercise 1.

3 Read the text again and answer the questions.

  1 How many rooms are there in the house altogether?

    seven

  2 Where does the writer spend a lot of time?

    _____

  3 What does the writer like looking at?

    _____

  4 What pets have the grandparents got?

    _____

  5 Who usually works in the garden?

    _____

  6 What does the grandfather do in the evening?

    _____

Vocabulary extension

4 Label the pictures with the highlighted words from the text.

1 *oven*

2 _____

3 _____

4 _____

5 _____

5 Complete the sentences with the words from Exercise 4.

  1 It's 9 a.m. Open the *curtains* so we can see the sun.

  2 Put the cake in the _____ for about 30 minutes.

  3 I sometimes fall asleep on this sofa because its _____ are very comfortable.

  4 In the UK, children believe that Santa Claus climbs down the _____.

  5 Sheila needs some new _____. She's got lots of books.

ACTIVE VOCABULARY | of /off

- We use *off* to mean 'away from a place'. It has the opposite meaning to *on*. We often use it in phrasal verbs (e.g. get **on**, get **off**).
- We often use *of* in expressions of quantity or to show a relationship between two things, people, etc. (e.g. *a bottle **of** water, stories **of** his life*).

6 Complete the sentences with *of* or *off*.

  1 There are lots **of** books on the table.

  2 I spend most _____ my time in the kitchen.

  3 I get _____ the bus at 8.45 a.m. and walk to school.

  4 I'd like a piece _____ cake.

  5 Sometimes our French teacher tells us stories _____ his time as a student in France.

  6 Take _____ your shoes before you come into the house.

  7 Switch _____ your phone. It's time for dinner.

7 ON A HIGH NOTE Write about a home that you really like and give reasons why.

UNIT VOCABULARY PRACTICE > page 25

We asked you where else you really feel at home apart from your own home. Here are some of your answers.

I feel completely at home in my grandparents' house. They live in a small village in the countryside. I like living in a town and I'm very happy in our apartment, but I love visiting my grandparents. As soon as I get off the train, I feel relaxed.

The house is quite old and very pretty. There are flowers all around it and, in winter, there is always smoke coming out of the chimney. Inside there are three bedrooms, a bathroom, a kitchen, a dining room and a living room. There aren't any stairs. It's only got one floor.

I spend most of my time in the living room. It's very clean and tidy. There is a big, comfortable sofa and an armchair. There are lots of cushions and it is easy to fall asleep, especially when there's a fire in the fireplace. My grandparents have big bookshelves full of old books. I love looking at them when I'm there. There are very thick, long curtains in the room. At night, when my grandparents close them, the room is quiet and warm. It's lovely.

My grandparents have got a small cupboard full of games. We often play them in the evening. My grandparents' animals, a cat and a dog, sit on our laps when we play the games. I haven't got any pets, so I love sitting with a dog or a cat on my lap.

Outside, there's a big garden where my grandfather grows vegetables. My grandmother loves cooking and there is always a hot dinner waiting for us in the oven. In the evening, my grandfather sits with us and tells us stories of his life. I'm not sure if they are all true but they are very interesting.

And that's why I really feel at home in my grandparents' house.

Leila

> Next article

2E LISTENING AND VOCABULARY

1 🔊 *9* **Listen to the conversation. What is the topic?**

  a a brother with annoying habits

  b how you feel when your brother leaves home

  c keeping your room tidy

2 🔊 *9* **Listen to the conversation again and choose the correct answers.**

  1 Why does Josh's brother sleep in his room?

    a His bedroom is now his dad's bedroom.

    b Josh wants him to stay in his room.

    c His bedroom isn't a bedroom now.

  2 What does Josh say about his brother and clothes?

    a There is nowhere for him to put them.

    b He often puts them in the wrong place.

    c He always leaves them on the floor.

  3 What does Josh say about his books?

    a His brother doesn't like them.

    b His brother makes notes in them.

    c His brother takes them to university.

  4 What is Katie's advice?

    a For Josh to talk to his brother about the problem.

    b For Katie to talk to Josh's brother.

    c For Josh not to worry so much about being tidy.

Vocabulary extension

3 **Match the words from the box, which you heard in the recording in Exercise 1, with the definitions.**

annoy ~~drawer~~ put away put back

  1 Part of a desk or a wardrobe that you pull out and push in and use to keep things in. _drawer_

  2 Make someone feel a bit angry and unhappy about something. _____

  3 Return something to the same place that you got it from. _____

  4 Put something in a wardrobe, cupboard, drawer when you are not using it. _____

4 🔊 *10* **Complete the extracts from the recording with the correct forms of the words from Exercise 3. Listen and check.**

  1 'And he reads my books.' 'That's OK, isn't it?' 'Yes, but he doesn't _put_ them _back_.'

  2 Make some suggestions about how you can live together and not _____ each other.

  3 He's got half a wardrobe and three _____ for his clothes.

  4 He doesn't _____ his things _____ or he puts them in the wrong place.

5 **ON A HIGH NOTE Do you share a bedroom with your brother or sister? If yes, write about the things you like or dislike about sharing a room. If no, write about the things you like or dislike about having your own room.**

Pronunciation

> ### ACTIVE PRONUNCIATION | Silent *h*
> We pronounce the letter *h* with a /h/ sound (e.g a **h**otel). In some words, *h* is silent (e.g. an **h**our).

6 🔊 *11* **Tick the words which contain a silent *h*. Listen, check and repeat.**

  1 ☐ how

  2 ☑ why

  3 ☐ what

  4 ☐ home

  5 ☐ his

  6 ☐ half

  7 ☐ hour

  8 ☐ him

7 🔊 *12* **Listen to some words containing a silent *h*. Write them correctly. Listen and repeat.**

  1 _wheel_

  2 _____

  3 _____

  4 _____

  5 _____

  6 _____

8 🔊 *13* **There are seven question words beginning with *wh*-. Write them in the correct column. Listen, check and repeat.**

Silent *h*	/h/ sound
what	

9 🔊 *14* **Sometimes two or more words sound the same but have a different spelling. Listen and choose the word you hear.**

I wanted a w**h**ole apple but there's a **h**ole in it.

  1 **h**our / our

  2 w**h**ere / wear

  3 w**h**ose / who's

  4 w**h**ole / **h**ole

  5 **h**our / our

  6 wea**th**er / w**h**e**th**er

1 🔊 *15* **Listen and repeat the phrases. How do you say them in your language?**

> ### SPEAKING | Asking for information
>
> **Can you give me some information about** the flat for rent?
>
> **How many** bathrooms are there?
>
> **Is there** a shower?
>
> **Has the flat got** a garden?
>
> **Can we** cook outside?
>
> **What do you mean by** 'small'?
>
> **Have you got** a dishwasher?

2 **Match the two parts of the questions.**

1. ☐ Has the house
2. ☐ What do you mean
3. ☐ How many
4. ☐ Can we
5. ☐ Have you got
6. ☐ Can you give me
7. ☐ Is there a

a look at the house this evening?
b dishwasher in the kitchen?
c got a dining room?
d a desk in your room?
e by 'traditional'?
f your phone number?
g bedrooms are there?

3 **Put the words in order to make questions.**

1. balcony / I / the / can / at / look / ?
   Can I look at the balcony?

2. garage / house / a / the / got / has / ?
   _____

3. wardrobe / got / you / a / big / have / ?
   _____

4. the / give / about / house / some / you / information / me / can / ?
   _____

5. bedrooms / there / many / are / how / ?
   _____

6. 'old' / mean / do / by / what / you / ?
   _____

7. a / there / machine / washing / is / ?
   _____

4 **Read the answers and complete the questions.**

1. *Is there a* study?
   No, there isn't.

2. _____ some information about your company?
   Yes, of course. Here's our brochure.

3. _____ are there?
   There are three bedrooms.

4. _____ stairs?
   No, there aren't. Everything is on one floor.

5. _____ by 'quiet area'?
   I mean that the road is quiet and the neighbours don't have parties.

6. _____ house _____ a new roof?
   Yes, it has. The roof is one year old.

7. _____ I go up to the attic?
   No, I'm sorry. It's dangerous.

5 **USE OF ENGLISH Complete the dialogue with one word in each gap.**

Fiona Hi, Jamie.

Jamie So, this is your new house. It's great! ¹*Can* I come in and see it?

Fiona Of course, come in!

Jamie How ² _____ bedrooms are there?

Fiona Four. My parents' room, my room, Jack's room and an extra bedroom. Dad wants to make it his study.

Jamie Is ³ _____ a garden?

Fiona Yes, it's magical!

Jamie What do you ⁴ _____ by 'magical'?

Fiona I mean it's like from a fairy tale.

Jamie Wow! I want to see it! What about your bedroom? ⁵ _____ you got a big room?

Fiona It isn't very big but it's OK. I've got a desk, a big wardrobe and a nice bed.

Jamie ⁶ _____ the house got wi-fi?

Fiona Of course! It's really quick too.

2G WRITING | A description of a place

Start with a general description of the room.

Describe the room in more detail. Include the furniture and parts of the room.

Mention your hobby/interest.

Use prepositions of place, adjectives and linkers.

Say why you like your room.

What's your dream bedroom like?

My dream bedroom is in a house in Los Angeles and the people in the house ¹<u>next</u> to mine are film stars! The room is big and modern. It's very light because ² _____ are big windows on one side of it. There's a beautiful view from the windows because I ³ _____ see the sea.

There's an enormous bed in my bedroom. The walls are yellow and there are lots of posters and maps on them. There are shelves with books on them above my bed and there's a desk with a computer, big speakers and lots of video games. Opposite the bed, there are two armchairs ⁴ _____ a sofa. My friends come to see me in the evening and we sit and listen to music and play video games. There's a fridge in the room too. It's got lots of good food in it and there's a balcony with a barbecue ⁵ _____ I can cook for my friends.

I love my dream bedroom because it's big and ⁶ _____.

---

1 Read the description and answer the questions.

  1 Which city is the writer's house in? <u>Los Angeles</u>
  2 What adjective describes the room and the windows?
  _____
  3 What can the writer see from the bedroom?
  _____
  4 What colour are the walls? _____
  5 What has the writer got on the walls? _____
  6 Where can the writer cook? _____

2 Complete the description with the words from the box.

and   can   comfortable   ~~next~~   so   there

3 Find the words in the description that match these definitions.

  1 An adjective to describe the room. m<u>odern</u>
  2 A preposition of position. a_____
  3 A Present Simple verb, the opposite of stand. s_____
  4 A part of a house. b_____
  5 An item of furniture. a_____
  6 An adjective meaning 'very big'. e_____
  7 Two linking words. b_____, s_____

4 Complete the description below with the words from Exercise 3.

5 WRITING TASK **Think of your dream room. Use the information below and your imagination to write a description.**

ACTIVE WRITING | A description of a place

1 **Plan your description.**
  • Think of a general description of the room: *big, modern, light*, etc.
  • Make notes about furniture and more adjectives you can use.
  • Think of prepositions of place you can use to describe where things are.
  • Think about a conclusion and your opinion about the room.

2 **Write the description.**
  • Use three paragraphs to organise your description.
  • Use *there is/there are* to say what is in the room.
  • Use prepositions of place to say where things are.
  • Use *and, but, because* and *so* to link your ideas together.

3 **Check that ...**
  • you have included all the relevant information.
  • there are no spelling or grammar mistakes.

We are on holiday in a house by the sea.

It isn't a ¹<u>modern</u> house, it's very old. It looks beautiful and I love everything except my room.

In my room, there's a small bed. It isn't comfortable. ² _____ the bed, I can see a spider on the ceiling! It's ³ _____! About 5 cm long with long legs. I haven't got

a lamp in my room ⁴ _____ it's very dark.

In the evenings I ⁵ _____ in the living room ⁶ _____ there's a very comfortable ⁷ _____ there.

Mum and dad love the house. They've got a warm bedroom with a ⁸ _____ outside. They go there in the evening and look at the view of the sea.

1 2A GRAMMAR AND VOCABULARY **Complete the text with one word in each gap.**

A room usually has four **¹**w*alls*, a **²**f_____ to walk on and a **³**c_____ above. There are usually **⁴**_____ to look out of and a **⁵**d_____ to close and open the room. Most homes have a **⁶**_____ where people cook, a **⁷**b_____ to wash in, a **⁸**b_____ to sleep in, and a **⁹**l_____ r_____ to relax in. Some homes have **¹⁰**s_____ to go up and down but some homes don't have them. Buildings also have a **¹¹**r_____ at the top, a **¹²**g_____ where you can park your car and a **¹³**b_____ or **¹⁴**t_____ so you can sit outside on a warm day.

2 2B VOCABULARY **Find the words which don't complete the sentences correctly.**

1 Come in and sit on the *sofa / armchair / sink*.
2 You can wash your hair in the *washbasin / washing machine / shower*.
3 I want to have a *mirror / rug / carpet* on the living room floor.
4 We wash the dishes in the *dishwasher / washing machine / sink*.
5 Put the food in the *fireplace / fridge / cupboard*.
6 We cook our dinner in the *microwave / cooker / shelf*.

3 2B VOCABULARY **Complete the sentences with the prepositions from the box.**

behind   between   front   next   on   under

1 There's a window *behind* the sofa.
2 All my books are _____ the shelves in my bedroom.
3 The cellar is _____ the kitchen.
4 In our house, the cooker is _____ the fridge and the sink.
5 The armchair is _____ to the lamp so it's a good place to sit and read.
6 The TV is in _____ of the sofa so we sit there to watch films.

4 2C GRAMMAR AND VOCABULARY **Match the two parts of the phrases. Use some of the words twice.**

1 ☐ iron   a the floor
2 ☐ vacuum   b dinner
3 ☐ keep   c the washing up
4 ☐ wash and dry   d the room tidy
5 ☐ sweep   e the clothes
6 ☐ do
7 ☐ cook

5 2D READING AND VOCABULARY **Complete the sentences with the opposites of the adjectives in bold.**

1 This room is really *messy*. You should tidy it. **TIDY**
2 It's nice and _____ in here with the fire on. **COLD**
3 Can you get some milk? This bottle is _____. **FULL**
4 When it gets _____, we switch the lights on. **LIGHT**
5 We live in a _____ road with lots of cars and buses. **QUIET**
6 This is an _____ bed. I don't like it. **COMFORTABLE**
7 This house is very _____. We often vacuum the floors and wash the windows. **DIRTY**
8 I like _____ furniture, not old chairs and tables. **TRADITIONAL**

6 2E LISTENING AND VOCABULARY **Complete the dialogue with *do* or *make*.**

Woman   Hello. Have you got five minutes to **¹**do a short questionnaire?

Teenager OK.

Woman   Great! I want you to give me a number from one to five for each question. One means 'not at all', five means 'yes, very'. Is that clear?

Teenager Yes, that's fine.

Woman   How easy is it for you to **²**_____ friends?

Teenager Oh, very easy. That's a five.

Woman   Do you **³**_____ a lot of mess in your room?

Teenager No, I'm quite tidy. I think that's a two.

Woman   How often do you **⁴**_____ suggestions to friends about how to change their lives?

Teenager Sometimes. I talk to them about clothes. Three, for that.

Woman   OK. Finally, do you always **⁵**_____ your best at school?

Teenager Not always but usually. Can I say three and a half?

Woman   No, sorry. Three or four.

Teenager OK, four.

Woman   Right. That's it. Thank you very much for your help.

7 ON A HIGH NOTE **Describe your dream holiday house. Say what rooms there are in the house and what is in each one. Use prepositions of position and adjectives to say where things are and what the house is like.**

1 **For each learning objective, write 1–5 to assess your ability.**

1 = I don't feel confident. 5 = I feel confident.

	Learning objective	Course material	How confident I am (1–5)
2A	I can use *there is/there are* and *some/any* to talk about my home.	Student's Book pp. 24–25 Workbook pp. 16–17	
2B	I can talk about rooms, furniture and the location of things in a house.	Student's Book p. 26 Workbook p. 18	
2C	I can use *can* and *can't* to talk about household chores.	Student's Book p. 27 Workbook p. 19	
2D	I can predict what the text is about and talk about houses.	Student's Book pp. 28–29 Workbook pp. 20–21	
2E	I can identify specific information in an interview and talk about roommates.	Student's Book p. 30 Workbook p. 22	
2F	I can ask for information about a house or flat.	Student's Book p. 31 Workbook p. 23	
2G	I can write a description of a place.	Student's Book p. 32 Workbook p. 24	

2 **Which of the skills above would you like to improve in? How?**

Skill I want to improve in	How I can improve

3 **What can you remember from this unit?**

New words I learned and most want to remember	Expressions and phrases I liked	English I heard or read outside class

GRAMMAR AND VOCABULARY

1 Choose the correct words to match the definitions.

1 It's something you can put books on.
   shelf / wall

2 It's the room at the top of the house.
   attic / cellar

3 It's where you put your clothes.
   garage / wardrobe

4 It's for two, three or four people.
   armchair / sofa

5 It's for cleaning clothes.
   dishwasher / washing machine

         / 5

2 Match sentence beginnings 1–5 with endings a–h. There are three extra endings.

1 ☐ We can eat at the breakfast	**a** up.
2 ☐ My parents have got a double	**b** floor.
3 ☐ You can help me do the washing	**c** dishes.
4 ☐ Every Saturday I sweep or vacuum the	**d** view.
5 ☐ Put the milk in the	**e** fridge.
	f bed.
	g bar.
	h balcony.

         / 5

3 Put the words in order to make sentences.

1 class / people / your / many / in / there / are / how / ?
   How many people are there in your class?

2 living / any / our / room / aren't / in / books / there
   _____

3 animals / draw / of / you / pictures / can / ?
   _____

4 writing / can't / my / teachers / read / my
   _____

5 the / in / any / cellar / are / windows / there / ?
   _____

6 Italian / dad / food / cook / my / can
   _____

         / 5

4 Read the questions and write the answers.

1 Is there a washing machine in the kitchen?
   ✓ *Yes, there is.*

2 Can your friends play a musical instrument?
   ✗ _____

3 Can your sister drive?
   ✗ _____

4 Are there any cars in the garage?
   ✗ _____

5 Can you write a description of your bedroom?
   ✓ _____

6 Is there a sofa in the living room?
   ✓ _____

         / 5

USE OF ENGLISH

5 Choose the correct words a–d to complete the text.

ROOM FOR ¹__

Good for students.

Good location in a ²__ part of the city.
Nice ³__ next door who are always happy to help.
Buses to the centre every 10 minutes.

⁴__ three rooms with two beds in each room.
Each room has a desk and a ⁵__ for clothes.

£600 a month so you can share the rooms and
pay just £100 each!

Tel: 0231 3214839

1 **a** rent	**b** move	**c** share	**d** relax
2 **a** dirty	**b** light	**c** quiet	**d** noisy
3 **a** roommates	**b** apartment	**c** friends	**d** neighbours
4 **a** There are	**b** Are there	**c** There is	**d** Is there
5 **a** carpet	**b** fridge	**c** wardrobe	**d** garage

         / 5

6 Complete the sentences with the correct words formed from the verbs in bold.

1 We can eat in the *dining* room. **DINE**

2 I need to clean my room. It's so _____ that I can't find anything! **MESS**

3 I need a more _____ chair. I can't sit on this one! **COMFORT**

4 In a _____ Japanese bathroom there's a big bath to relax in. **TRADITION**

5 Can you give me some _____ about the house, please? **INFORM**

6 I need some _____ about the colour of my bedroom walls. **SUGGEST**

         / 5

         / 30

03 Eat in – eat out

3A GRAMMAR AND VOCABULARY

Countable and uncountable nouns with *some/any/no*

1 ★ Which words are countable and which are uncountable? Find the odd one out in each group.

1 beef   rice   coffee   (tomato)
2 bread   biscuit   crisp   egg
3 butter   cake   sandwich   chocolate
4 spinach   potato   yoghurt   cheese
5 juice   tea   ice cream   sardine
6 tuna   apple   pasta   cereal

2 ★ Match the two parts of the sentences.

A
1 ☐ There is   **a** any bread.
2 ☐ There isn't   **b** any eggs.
3 ☐ There aren't   **c** no butter.

B
1 ☐ Is there an   **a** cake?
2 ☐ Are there any   **b** apple?
3 ☐ Is there any   **c** apples?

C
1 ☐ There isn't   **a** some cereal.
2 ☐ There is   **b** any pasta.
3 ☐ There are   **c** no potatoes.

3 ★ Choose the correct words to complete the sentences.

1 Are there __ biscuits?
   a some   **b** a   **c** any
2 Have you got __ milk?
   a any   **b** a   **c** some
3 There isn't __ yoghurt.
   a no   **b** some   **c** any
4 There's __ beef in the shop.
   a any   **b** no   **c** a
5 Have we got __ egg?
   a no   **b** any   **c** an
6 We need __ pasta.
   a a   **b** any   **c** some
7 Oh, no! There are __ crisps left!
   a any   **b** no   **c** a
8 Don't buy __ tomatoes. We've got some at home.
   a some   **b** a   **c** any

4 ★ Complete the dialogue with *how much* or *how many*.

Mel I hate shopping.
Dan Me too. Let's be quick. Here's the shopping list. You get these things, OK?
Mel OK but ¹*how much* beef do you want?
Dan About one kilo.
Mel And ²_____ butter?
Dan About 250 g.
Mel ³_____ eggs do you want? Six or twelve?
Dan Get twelve. Right, see you in a minute.
Mel Wait! ⁴_____ apples do you want?
Dan I don't know. Four?
Mel OK, one last thing. ⁵_____ chocolate do you want?
Dan Chocolate? There isn't any chocolate on the list.
Mel I know but I'm hungry and I want to eat something before we get home.

5 ★★ USE OF ENGLISH Complete the second sentence using the word in bold so that it means the same as the first one. Use no more than three words, including the word in bold.

1 There is no tea. **ANY**
   There *isn't any* tea.
2 There isn't any spinach. **NO**
   There _____ spinach.
3 There are no sardines. **ANY**
   There _____ sardines.
4 There is no cheese. **ANY**
   There _____ cheese.
5 There aren't any crisps. **NO**
   There _____ crisps.

6 ★★ Complete the sentences with the words from the box.

a   an   any   are   aren't   many   much   no   ~~some~~

1 There is *some* butter but there isn't _____ bread.
2 I've got _____ apple but I haven't got _____ potato.
3 How _____ fruit and how _____ vegetables do you eat every day?
4 There _____ any crisps for the party but there _____ some biscuits.
5 There are _____ eggs in the fridge. Not one!

7 ★★ Use the prompts to write sentences with *some*, *any*, *much* and *many*.

1 How / chicken / there?
How much chicken is there?
2 I / got / water but / not / got / juice
_____
3 you / got / sugar?
_____
4 There / not / cheese
_____
5 there / meat?
_____
6 How / eggs / you / want?
_____
7 There / some / sardines but / there / any / tuna
_____
8 there / apples?
_____
9 We / not / got / milk
_____

8 ★★★ Read the answers and complete the questions.

1 *How many eggs have you* got?
We've got three eggs.
2 _____ juice?
Yes, there is. Do you want some?
3 _____ got?
We've got about a kilo of rice.
4 _____ meat?
Yes, there is. There's some beef and some chicken.
5 _____ vegetables in the kitchen?
No, there aren't.
6 _____ tea?
No, I haven't but I've got some coffee.

9 ★★★ USE OF ENGLISH Complete the dialogue with one word in each gap.

Ali   Mum wants some sandwiches for the picnic this afternoon. Can you help?
Danielle Yes, of course. Have you got **1***any* bread?
Ali   Yes, here it is.
Danielle There's **2**_____ butter in the fridge.
Ali   I know. It's on the table.
Danielle **3**_____ there any meat?
Ali   **4**_____ is some chicken but my mum doesn't eat meat.
Danielle OK, no problem. There **5**_____ some eggs here. I can cook them and make egg sandwiches.
Ali   How **6**_____ eggs do you want to cook?
Danielle Three or four.

Later ...
Danielle OK, the sandwiches are ready.
Ali   Great. And we've got two apples and **7**_____ crisps. We just need juice now.
Danielle How **8**_____ do you want?
Ali   Two litres.
Danielle There we are.
Ali   Thanks. There's **9**_____ bag on the cupboard. We can put it all in there.

10 ON A HIGH NOTE Imagine you're going on a picnic. Make a list of the food and drink you would take with you.

UNIT VOCABULARY PRACTICE > page 37   29

3B VOCABULARY | Containers, prices

1 ★ Complete the names of containers with a vowel (a, e, i, o, u) in each gap.

1 t_i_n
2 b___x
3 j___r
4 b___g
5 c___n
6 c___rt___n
7 b___ttl___
8 p___ck___t

2 ★★ Complete the shopping list with the names of containers from Exercise 1.

> 1 a _bottle_ of water
> 2 a _____ of tuna
> 3 four _____ of crisps
> 4 a _____ of mayonnaise
> 5 two _____ of juice
> 6 a _____ of sweets
> 7 two _____ of coke
> 8 a _____ of chocolates

3 ★★ Complete the dialogue with the prices in words.

Marina Water is ¹_forty-nine pence_ (49p) a bottle so four bottles are ² _____ (£1.96).

Neil That's OK. How much is chocolate?

Marina This is ³_____ (60p) but it isn't very nice. We can get some good chocolate for ⁴_____ (£1.15).

Neil Yes, good idea. Mum wants some oil but this is ⁵_____ (£5.25)!

Marina Don't worry. We can get some good oil for ⁶_____ (£2.20). Here. Is that it?

Neil Yes. So that's ...⁷_____ (£5.31), I think. I've only got ⁸_____ (£4.50). Have you got ⁹_____ (81p) you can give me?

Marina Yes, here you are. Here's a pound.

4 ★★★ Look at the picture and use the words from the box to make a list of products with the container, the name of the food and the price in words.

biscuits chocolates coffee milk ~~oil~~ tuna

1 A _bottle of oil_ – _one pound twenty-nine_
2 A _____ – _____
3 A _____ – _____
4 A _____ – _____
5 A _____ – _____
6 A _____ – _____

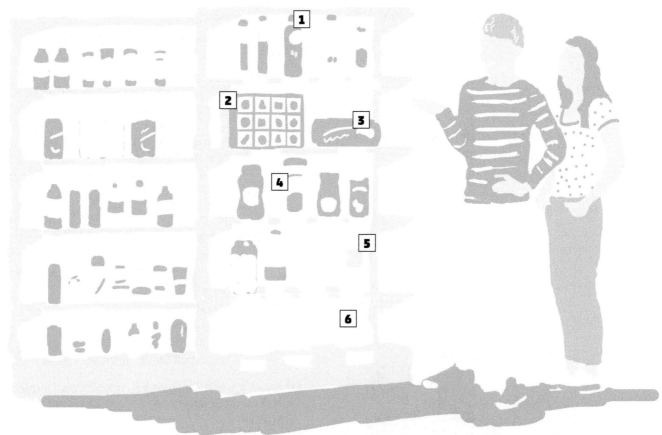

5 ON A HIGH NOTE **Write about the food that you sometimes buy. What does it come in (packet, tin, etc.) and how much does it cost in British pounds?**

3C SPEAKING

1 🔊 16 Listen and repeat the phrases. How do you say them in your language?

SPEAKING | Ordering food

TAKING ORDERS

How can I help you?
Are you ready to order?
What would you like to eat/drink?
Would you like any cake or desserts?
Anything else?
Anything to drink?
Is that all?
That's £21.50, please.
You're welcome.

GIVING ORDERS

Can I have a tuna salad, **please?**
I'd like a chicken sandwich/**some** tea, **please.**
Yes, I want a cheese sandwich, **please.**
How much is that?
Here you are.
Thank you.

2 Put the words in order to make sentences. Then write S for the server and C for the customer.

1 can / you / how / help / I / ?
   [S] *How can I help you?*
2 order / you / to / are / ready / ?
   ☐ _____
3 much / that / how / is / ?
   ☐ _____
4 salad / I / have / can / please / a / chicken / ?
   ☐ _____
5 like / would / desserts / you / any / ?
   ☐ _____
6 please / like / some / I'd / cake / chocolate
   ☐ _____

3 Complete the dialogue with one word in each gap.

Server Anything ¹*else*?
Customer Yes, I'd ² _____ a glass of juice, please.
Server Is that ³ _____?
Customer Yes, thanks.
Server That's £12.80, please.
Customer ⁴ _____ you are.
Customer Thank you.
Server You're ⁵ _____.

4 Choose the correct responses to complete the mini-conversations.

1
Server How can I help you?
Customer __
a Yes, please. I'd like a drink.
b You're welcome.
c Can I have a chicken sandwich, please?

2
Customer __
Server You're welcome.
a Here you are.
b How much is that?
c Thank you very much.

3
Server Are you ready to order?
Customer __
a Yes, I want a cheese sandwich, please.
b Yes, here you are.
c Yes, is that all?

4
Customer How much is that?
Server __
a That's £8.50, please.
b You're welcome.
c Here you are.

5 Complete the dialogue with responses a–e.

Server Hi. Are you ready to order something to eat?
Customer ¹*e*
Server OK. Anything to drink?
Customer ² __
Server Is that all?
Customer ³ __
Server That's £6.50, please.
Customer ⁴ __
Server Here's your food and drink.
Customer ⁵ __
Server You're welcome. Enjoy your meal.

a Here you are.
b Yes, thanks. How much is that?
c A cup of green tea, please.
d Thanks a lot.
e ~~Yes, can I have a cheese salad, please?~~

3D GRAMMAR

Quantifiers: *a lot of, too many, too much, a few, a little, not many, not much*

1 ⭐ **Choose the correct words to complete the sentences.**

1 I've got *a lot of / many* pasta.

2 There isn't *many / much* sugar in this cake.

3 There is a *little / few* milk. I think we can have a cup of coffee.

4 There are too *many / much* potatoes. We've got five for each person!

5 We haven't got *much / many* eggs so we can't make a Spanish omelette.

6 There are a *little / few* tomatoes so we can make a salad.

2 ⭐⭐ **Complete the sentences with the correct words in bold. There is one extra word for each sentence.**

FEW / MANY / MUCH

1 We haven't got <u>*much*</u> bread, but we can make a <u>*few*</u> sandwiches.

LOT / NOT / TOO

2 There's _____ much milk left so don't put _____ much in your coffee.

FEW / LITTLE / LOT

3 There's a _____ of rice but only a _____ meat. We can add some vegetables and make a Chinese meal.

LOT / TOO / MANY

4 You've got a _____ of chips. I haven't got _____. Can I have some of yours?

LOT / MUCH / MANY

5 Do you think there's too _____ salt in this soup? Well, there is quite a _____ but it's OK.

FEW / LITTLE / TOO

6 We've got a _____ biscuits, but there are _____ many people here to give them one biscuit each.

3 ⭐⭐ **Complete the dialogue with the words from the box. You can use some words more than once.**

few   little   lot   many   much   of

Tom   So, doctor. What do you think?

Doctor   I think you eat too **1** <u>*many*</u> sweets and too **2** _____ chocolate. Also, you don't eat **3** _____ fruit and you don't eat **4** _____ vegetables.

Tom   I always have a **5** _____ carrots for lunch.

Doctor   Very good but you also eat a **6** _____ of bread and meat and you don't drink **7** _____ water.

Tom   I drink a **8** _____. A glass a day.

Doctor   You need four glasses a day. So, eat a lot **9** _____ fruit and vegetables and only a **10** _____ meat. And no sweets or chocolates. Come back and see me in a month.

Tom   OK, thank you.

4 ⭐⭐ **Use the prompts to write sentences about the pictures.**

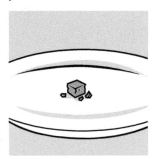

1 There / little / cheese
<u>*There is a little cheese.*</u>

2 There / lot / crisps
_____

3 There / lot / bread
_____

4 There / much / milk
_____

5 There / many / chips
_____

6 There / too / tea
_____

5 ⭐⭐⭐ **USE OF ENGLISH Complete the text with one word in each gap.**

Not many of my friends have a hot lunch at school. Most of us have sandwiches. A **1** <u>*few*</u> people have biscuits or crisps for lunch but not **2** _____. Most people want to be healthy so a **3** _____ of my friends bring things like a small yoghurt and an apple to school. Sometimes, we put our lunch on the table and we take a **4** _____ food from each person. One boy always has a big bag of crisps, so we all take a **5** _____ because there are **6** _____ many for him. I usually have too **7** _____ bread so one friend takes one of my sandwiches. It's a great idea and we never waste any food – well **8** _____ much anyway.

6 ON A HIGH NOTE **Describe lunchtime at your school. Is there a canteen? What kind of food can you get there? What do you and your friends eat and drink?**

3E LISTENING AND VOCABULARY

1 Complete the text with the words from the box.

taste ~~taster~~ tasters tastes tasty

A food **1** *taster* is a person who **2**_____ different kinds of new food. If the person thinks the food is **3**_____, they say that it's good. If they don't like the **4**_____ of the food, they say that it's bad. If a lot of food **5**_____ say that they like the food, the company can start selling it.

2 🔊 **17** Listen to the interview and answer the questions.

1 How often does Amber do food tasting?
about once a month

2 What does Amber compare food tasting to?
_____

3 How many items of food are there to try at each session?
_____

4 When does she get paid?
_____

3 🔊 **17** Listen to the interview again and complete the notes with one to four words.

1 Amber can't taste food with *cheese* in it.

2 The food comes in plates and bowls made of _____.

3 Between different items of food, they have a _____.

4 One session takes about _____.

5 For one tasting, Amber earns _____.

Vocabulary extension

4 Match the words from the box, which you heard in the recording in Exercise 2, with the definitions.

disgusting form full up ~~invite~~ register sign

1 Ask someone if they want to go somewhere, e.g. a party. *invite*

2 Write your name on an official document. _____

3 Complete a document to join a website or other organisation. _____

4 Not nice at all, horrible. _____

5 Feeling like you can't eat any more. _____

6 A document with questions to answer and information to add. _____

5 ON A HIGH NOTE Write about the food you like the taste of and the food that you don't like the taste of.

Pronunciation

> ### ACTIVE PRONUNCIATION | /uː/ and /ʊ/ sounds
> English has long and short vowel sounds.
> • long sound /uː/ (e.g. f**oo**d)
> • short sound /ʊ/ (e.g. g**oo**d)
> Be careful, the letters *oo* can make /ʊ/ or /uː/.

6 🔊 **18** Listen and repeat. Then write the words in the correct column.

/uː/	/ʊ/
food	good

7 🔊 **19** The /uː/ sound can be made by different combinations of vowels, not just *oo*. Listen to twelve words and repeat them. Then complete the table.

oo	ue	ou	u	ui	ew
spoon					

8 🔊 **20** The /ʊ/ sound can also be spelled with different vowels. Listen to three pairs of words and write them down. What vowels represent the /ʊ/ sound in each pair of words?

1 *wolf* _____   **2** _____   **3** _____
_____   _____   _____

9 🔊 **21** Listen and find the word that has a different vowel sound to the other words in each group. Listen again and repeat.

1 food (cook) pool
2 full put music
3 roof balloon good
4 afternoon cook look
5 fruit butcher juice
6 foot queue tuna

3F READING AND VOCABULARY

1 Read the text quickly and match headings A–E with paragraphs 1–5.

A A strange idea?

B How to attract customers

C Successful despite the location

D Something for everyone

E Inside the restaurant

2 Read the text again and choose the correct answers.

1 What do we find out about restaurants in London?

  a Restaurants with good food are always successful.

  b There aren't many restaurants with interesting design.

  c It is difficult for restaurants to be successful.

  d There aren't many restaurants in London.

2 What is true about The Schoolhouse restaurant?

  a All the notices on the walls make people laugh.

  b You can see photographs of some of the people who eat there.

  c The restaurant uses real school desks for the tables.

  d Customers can read books in the restaurant.

3 Why do so many people like The Schoolhouse?

  a Because they have good memories of their school dinners.

  b Because it is cheaper than other places to eat.

  c Because the waiters are unusually friendly.

  d Because it's an unusual place for a restaurant.

4 Which of these does the writer NOT mention?

  a A collection of smaller portions that two people eat together.

  b Food from different parts of the world.

  c Food for people who don't want to eat much.

  d Food which is a speciality of the restaurant.

5 What does the author think about The Schoolhouse?

  a The location sounds ideal.

  b It is an expensive place to eat.

  c There isn't a good choice of food.

  d The restaurant sounds interesting.

Vocabulary extension

3 Complete the sentences with the highlighted words from the text.

1 We want to eat out today. One *option* is pizza, and another is an Indian takeaway.

2 This restaurant is quite _____. People sit and eat in the dark.

3 The only thing my brother can cook is a _____ egg!

4 I'm not very hungry so I just want a _____ snack.

5 This restaurant serves many vegetarian _____. You can order hummus or a veggie burger.

6 People come here for the food but also for the _____ service. The waiters are the best in London.

ACTIVE VOCABULARY | Homophones

Homophones are words which have a different meaning and spelling but sound the same (e.g. *meat*, *meet*).

4 🔊 **22** Listen and complete the sentences with the homophones from the box.

flour / flower	~~meat / meet~~	pair / pear
peace / piece	there / their	where / wear

1 a What time do you want to *meet*?

  b I don't eat *meat* but I eat fish and other seafood.

2 a Oh, a _____, thank you. It's beautiful.

  b To make the cake, you need _____, eggs and butter.

3 a What should I _____ when I go out with Lucy?

  b _____ are the eggs? I need one.

4 a I need some _____ and quiet after a long day teaching.

  b Would you like a _____ of my chocolate cake?

5 a I've got a new _____ of trousers. Do you want to see them?

  b I haven't got an apple but I've got a _____.

6 a Malcolm and Louise want to open _____ new restaurant on Saturday.

  b _____ is a cake in the kitchen. Who is it for?

5 ON A HIGH NOTE Write if you prefer to eat in or out. Explain why.

UNUSUAL PLACES TO *eat out* IN LONDON

1 ☐ There are a lot of different restaurants in London. This means that they have to try harder to fill all the tables and make money. It isn't easy. In order to be successful, restaurants need to offer more than just good food and excellent service. That's why London is full of unusual restaurants that combine good food with interesting designs. Here are some of our favourites.

The Schoolhouse

2 ☐ The first thing you notice when you walk inside The Schoolhouse restaurant is that it looks like a real school. There are books on shelves, locked behind glass doors. There are notices on the walls. Some are funny, others educational. There is also a collection of photos, not of students and teachers, but of customers who post them on the restaurant's social media pages. Have a look round and then sit down at one of the wooden tables, which are specially designed to look like old-fashioned school desks.

3 ☐ When adults in Britain think about their school dinners, they don't usually have pleasant thoughts. Burnt meat, hard bread and fried potatoes cooked in old oil. So, at first, it is surprising that The Schoolhouse is so popular. The waiters are helpful and the prices are not too high, but that's true for many other restaurants. So, why do so many people choose to eat here? Many of them come here because of the building, which makes the experience more special than a normal meal out.

4 ☐ Fortunately, the food in The Schoolhouse is not like school dinners at all. There are meals for meat lovers and vegetarians, people who are very hungry and people who just want a light snack. You can choose Mexican meals with delicious red beans, British fish and chips, Italian pasta or other dishes. The friendly waiters are happy to help you decide. One option is a sharing plate for two people with lots of different small dishes that you can enjoy together. I can definitely recommend it.

5 ☐ The Schoolhouse is on a busy, south London street, far away from the tourist attractions and not somewhere most people would walk past. It isn't easy to run a successful restaurant in an area like that but, obviously, the idea of eating in a building that looks like a school canteen is a good one.

The Rainforest café ›

Write the name and the style of the café.

Describe the café and say why people like it.

Mention the menu and your favourite dish, and say what you particularly like about the café.

Say where it is and give the opening hours.

The Laundromat Café in Copenhagen, Denmark is a great place for people who have a lot of housework to do. inside the café there is a room with comfortable sofas and armchairs as well as washing machines so you can sit and relax while you do your washing. It also has play areas for children, Newspapers, magazines and even games to play.

I like it because i am a student and I can go there in the evening to wash my clothes and use the free Internet. I like their coffee and their delicious cakes.

There are now three Laundromat Cafés in denmark, two in Copenhagen and one in frederiksberg. The one I go to is on arhusgade street. It is open every day from 9 a.m. to 9 p.m. even on sundays.

1 Read the review and complete the notes.

Name of café: ¹*The Laundromat Café*
Where it is: ² _____
Food and drink: ³ _____
Opening hours: Days: ⁴ _____
Time: ⁵ _____

2 Find seven mistakes with capitals in the review and match them with reasons a–g.

1 ☐ *inside*
2 ☐ _____
3 ☐ _____
4 ☐ _____
5 ☐ _____
6 ☐ _____
7 ☐ _____

a New sentences start with a capital letter.
b Street names need a capital letter.
c Days of the week need a capital letter.
d Names of countries need a capital letter.
e The pronoun *I* needs a capital letter.
f Names of cities need a capital letter.
g Nouns in the middle of sentences don't have a capital letter.

3 Rewrite the sentences to make them correct.

1 My favourite café is Café El Time on la palma in the Canary Islands.
My favourite café is Café El Time on La Palma in the Canary Islands.

2 there is a great view of the beach and the town of tazacorte from the café.
_____

3 it is open every day until Eight o'clock in the evening.
_____

4 My friends and i often go there after school on fridays.
_____

5 My cousin sophia likes to walk to the café from School, but I go by bus.
_____

4 WRITING TASK **Think about a great snack bar – one you know or imagine one – and write a review of it.**

ACTIVE WRITING | A café review

1 Plan your review.
  • Think of a name and a style of the snack bar.
  • Think about why people like it.
  • Make notes of some ideas of food and drink that the snack bar sells.
  • Decide where it is and its opening hours.

2 Write the review.
  • Use three or four paragraphs to organise your review.
  • Use food and drink vocabulary to describe the menu.
  • Use adjectives to describe the snack bar.
  • Use capital letters where necessary.

3 Check that ...
  • you have included all the relevant information.
  • there are no spelling or grammar mistakes.

1 3A GRAMMAR AND VOCABULARY **Choose two words that fit each category.**

1 MEAT

(beef) rice tuna (chicken)

2 FRUIT

apples spinach lettuce bananas

3 FISH

chips pasta sardines tuna

4 VEGETABLES

tomatoes potatoes cheese bread

5 DAIRY FOOD

yoghurt juice butter cereal

6 DRINKS

crisps cake tea milk

2 3B VOCABULARY **Complete the text with the words from the box. There are two extra words.**

bottle box cans fresh jar ~~list~~ oil packets tins

Shopping ¹*list*

Two ² _____ of crisps

A ³ _____ of mayonnaise

Four ⁴ _____ of cola

Two ⁵ _____ of tuna

A ⁶ _____ of water

A ⁷ _____ of chocolates

3 3E LISTENING AND VOCABULARY **Complete the dialogue with one word in each gap.**

Eden So, are we ready for dinner?

Hallam I think so. We start with soup. We've got these nice ¹b*owls* to put the soup in and these ²s_____ to eat it with.

Eden They aren't for soup. They're for dessert. Here, put these on the table.

Hallam Oh, OK. What about this ³k_____. Is it OK for dinner?

Eden Yes, but why have you only got one?

Hallam The others are in the dishwasher.

Eden But the dishwasher isn't on. Take them out and wash them up in the sink. And wash some nice ⁴f_____ as well.

Hallam OK. And the ⁵p_____?

Eden Of course. We need them to put the food on. Now, what can we give people to drink?

Hallam Water, juice or cola.

Eden Great.

Hallam Where are the ⁶c_____?

Eden You mean, where are the ⁷g_____? It's Mum's 40ᵗʰ birthday and we want it to be special.

Hallam OK. How's the food?

Eden Let me worry about the food. You get the table ready.

4 3E LISTENING AND VOCABULARY **Match the people from the box with the comments they refer to.**

baker butcher chef dietician food photographer restaurant reviewer ~~waiter~~

1 He's useless. He always brings the wrong food to the table. *waiter*

2 I always read her opinions before I decide where to eat. _____

3 She gives really good advice about what to eat. _____

4 He cooks the most amazing pasta dishes. _____

5 Her bread is amazing. _____

6 I always look at her website. The food looks so delicious. _____

7 I like his shop because the meat is always fresh. _____

5 3F READING AND VOCABULARY **Choose the correct words to complete the sentences.**

1 I'd love to find __ what's in this soup.

a off **b** out **c** down

2 You can't just go in and sit __. Wait for the waiter to take us to our table.

a down **b** up **c** out

3 There are always people outside the new Mexican restaurant. They give __ leaflets to people when they walk past but I have never seen anyone in the restaurant.

a up **b** off **c** out

4 I asked my friends about the meal. Portia can help __ if we want.

a out **b** up **c** in

5 Don't give __. You can make bread. I know you can. Try one more time.

a out **b** off **c** up

6 There's nothing in the fridge, it's late and I'm hungry. Let's eat __ tonight.

a in **b** down **c** out

6 ON A HIGH NOTE **Write about the food you eat often, sometimes, rarely and never.**

1 For each learning objective, write 1–5 to assess your ability.

1 = I don't feel confident. 5 = I feel confident.

	Learning objective	Course material	How confident I am (1–5)
3A	I can use countable and uncountable nouns to talk about diets.	Student's Book pp. 38–39 Workbook pp. 28–29	
3B	I can talk about food products, containers and prices.	Student's Book p. 40 Workbook p. 30	
3C	I can order food and drinks in a café.	Student's Book pp. 40–41 Workbook p. 31	
3D	I can use quantifiers to talk about amounts.	Student's Book p. 42 Workbook p. 32	
3E	I can understand the main idea of a radio interview and talk about people and food.	Student's Book p. 43 Workbook p. 33	
3F	I can identify specific information in an article and talk about restaurants.	Student's Book pp. 44–45 Workbook pp. 34–35	
3G	I can write a café review.	Student's Book p. 46 Workbook p. 36	

2 Which of the skills above would you like to improve in? How?

Skill I want to improve in	How I can improve

3 What can you remember from this unit?

New words I learned and most want to remember	Expressions and phrases I liked	English I heard or read outside class

GRAMMAR AND VOCABULARY

1 Choose the correct words to complete the sentences.

1 Don't forget to buy a ___ of mayonnaise.
   a packet   **b** bag   **c** jar
2 I don't eat ___ because I'm a vegetarian.
   a beef   **b** rice   **c** spinach
3 There's an empty table. Let's sit ___ and look at the menu.
   a up   **b** out   **c** down
4 Can I have a ___ for my soup, please?
   a knife   **b** fork   **c** spoon
5 We always buy our meat from the local ___, not the supermarket.
   a butcher   **b** waiter   **c** baker

/ 5

2 Match sentence beginnings 1–5 with endings a–e.

1 ☐ When I finish school, I want to get a job as a restaurant
2 ☐ We haven't got much time, so, for lunch, we can open a tin of
3 ☐ I'd like a cup of
4 ☐ I don't want a main course. Just some chocolate ice
5 ☐ My favourite drink is orange

a juice.
b tea with milk, please.
c tuna.
d cream.
e reviewer.

/ 5

3 Complete the sentences with the words from the box. There are three extra words.

any   few   how   little   lot   many   ~~much~~   some   too

1 How *much* milk do you drink every week?
2 We need some cheese. We haven't got _____. Not even one gram!
3 We've got a _____ of bread. Do you want some toast?
4 I can't go out today. I've got _____ many things to do.
5 It isn't a big party – just a _____ friends.
6 There's _____ fish in the fridge. We can cook that.

/ 5

4 Choose the correct words to complete the text.

There are a **1**___ of restaurants in our town but only a **2**___ of them are popular with teenagers. The others are very expensive. There are **3**___ fast food bars but there is a Chinese takeaway and a great pizza place where we all meet on Fridays. There are **4**___ nice cafés but a coffee costs £2.50 which is **5**___ for me.

1 **a** few   **b** many   **c** lot
2 **a** little   **b** much   **c** few
3 **a** any   **b** no   **c** some
4 **a** few   **b** any   **c** some
5 **a** too much   **b** a lot of   **c** too many

/ 5

USE OF ENGLISH

5 Complete the messages with one word in each gap.

Hi, Luke!
Have a great time at college. Try not to go out too often. It's expensive. Don't worry if you can't cook. In my experience, other people always help **1***out*. You can make a nice meal with some eggs, a bag **2**_____ salad, bread and some mayonnaise.
Jim

Luke, enjoy your time at college. Your mum says you're worried about cooking. There are **3**_____ good websites with ideas for quick, easy, cheap meals. There are a lot of meals you can try – hundreds of them! Find **4**_____ how to cook – it's important!
Annie

Hey Luke,
I hear you want to know about working while at university. It's a good idea. Get a job **5**_____ a waiter in a restaurant. It's hard work carrying plates of food from the kitchen to the tables. At the weekends, restaurants are full and there is **6**_____ time for a break. But, when customers are happy with your work, they leave great tips – some people leave £5 or £10. And the restaurant gives you free food!
Hannah

/ 5

6 Complete the text with the correct words formed from the words in bold.

THE OLD MARKET CAFÉ REVIEW

This is a lovely restaurant. Their **1***speciality* (**SPECIAL**) is sea food and I recommend their fish soup as a **2**_____ (**START**). It really is delicious. There are also a lot of choices with no meat or fish so it's perfect for **3**_____ (**VEGETABLE**) too. If you're just a little **4**_____ (**HUNGER**), try their sandwiches. They're cheap, fresh and full of healthy ingredients.

They also bake their own delicious and beautiful looking cakes. They aren't the kind of thing a **5**_____ (**DIET**) would recommend but are great for people who like sweet things and even better for food **6**_____ (**PHOTOGRAPH**) trying to get perfect photos for their websites!

/ 5

/ 30

4A **GRAMMAR AND VOCABULARY**

Present Continuous

1 ⭐ Match the verbs from the box with the spelling rules.

do eat feel get have make put read run sit
stand stop swim take taste use wear write

1 Add -*ing*: <u>do</u>, _____, _____, _____,
_____, _____

2 Double the last letter and add -*ing*: _____,
_____, _____, _____, _____
_____

3 Remove the last letter and add -*ing*: _____,
_____, _____, _____, _____
_____

2 ⭐ Put the words in order to make sentences.

1 in / students / the / are / classroom / the / sitting
The students are sitting in the classroom.

2 to / talking / are / who / you / ?
_____

3 for / friends / waiting / my / I'm
_____

4 are / the / book / at / reading / moment / you / what / ?
_____

5 the / teacher / staff room / in / resting / our / is
_____

6 are / year / you / subjects / this / studying / what / ?
_____

3 ⭐ Read the questions and write short answers.

1 Are you working?
✓ *Yes, I am.*

2 Is your mum shopping?
✗ _____

3 Is your dad sleeping?
✓ _____

4 Is your sister watching TV?
✓ _____

5 Are you and your brother listening to music?
✗ _____

6 Are your friends playing football?
✓ _____

4 ⭐⭐ Complete the text with the correct Present Continuous forms of the verbs in brackets.

Welcome to this live video feed from our school. It's lunchtime. Here's the library. You can see some students. They ¹*are reading* (read). They ² _____ (not talk). You can't talk in the library. I can see a teacher. Oh, dear. She ³ _____ (ask) me to leave the library.

Outside, it ⁴ _____ (rain) but some students ⁵ _____ (run) in the playing fields. They run every day. I don't want to go and film them because I don't want my phone to get wet. We can go to the canteen. Some students ⁶ _____ (have) lunch. They ⁷ _____ (make) a lot of noise! Wait a minute. I can hear something. Some students ⁸ _____ (sing).

This is Mrs James. 'Hello, Mrs James. I ⁸ _____ (make) a film about our school. Do you want to say something?' No, she doesn't. She ¹⁰ _____ (go) away. I think she ¹¹ _____ (get) ready for this afternoon's lessons. And now the bell ¹² _____ (ring). It's time to finish. Thanks for watching.

5 ★★Use the prompts to complete the mini-conversations in the Present Continuous.

Carol Helen is sleeping.
Helen I / not / sleep. I / chat / with my friends
¹*I'm not sleeping. I'm chatting with my friends.*

Jack Matt and Bianca are listening to music.
Matt We / not / listen to music. We / sing
²_____

Mr Glover All the students are wearing uniforms today.
Mrs Evans No / not. Patrick / wear / jeans
³_____

Suzie Mum's reading a book.
Mum I / not / read a book. I / write / an email
⁴_____

Paul Why are you using your phone?
Me I / not / use my phone. I / wait / for a phone call
⁵_____

Cathy Are your parents driving to work?
Me No / not. They / walk / today
⁶_____

6 ★★Complete the text with the correct Present Continuous forms of the verbs from the box.

do enjoy look up show ~~sit~~ talk use watch write

This is a photo of my class. We **¹***are sitting* in our English classroom. Our teacher **²**_____ us a video. It's a film version of a book we're reading at the moment. A lot of people **³**_____ the video, but when you look closely, you might think that some people aren't interested, and **⁴**_____ other things. **⁵**I _____ in my notebook – but they are notes about the film. The boy next to me **⁶**_____ his phone. He **⁷**_____ a word from the video that he doesn't understand. Two girls **⁸**_____ – about the video. It's a very interesting video and we **⁹**_____ it.

7 ★★Use the prompts to write questions in the Present Continuous.

1 What / you / write?
What are you writing?

2 Where / Laura and Kira / go?
_____

3 What / your parents / watch?
_____

4 What / Mrs Underwood / draw?
_____

5 What sport / the students / play?
_____

6 Who / learn / English at the moment?
_____

8 ★★Use the prompts to write sentences in the Present Continuous. Then match them with questions 1–6 from Exercise 7.

a ☐ She / draw / a picture of the school
She's drawing a picture of the school.

b ☐ No one. Our English teacher / have / a break
_____

c ☐ I / write / an email
_____

d ☐ They / play / football
_____

e ☐ They / go / shopping
_____

f ☐ They / watch / a film
_____

9 ★★★Write sentences about the picture using the Present Continuous.

1 Mrs White *is drinking coffee*.
2 Clara _____.
3 Tom and Lucy _____.
4 Dominic _____.
5 Imelda and Nick _____.
6 Liam _____.

Tom and Lucy
Imelda and Nick
Mrs White
Liam
Clara
Dominic

10 ON A HIGH NOTE Write a few sentences about what you and your friends or members of your family are doing at the moment.

4B VOCABULARY | School subjects and classroom objects

1 ⭐ Complete the school subjects with one letter in each gap.

1 B i o l o g y
2 P__ __ s__ __ __ __ l E__ __ c__ __ __ __ __ n
3 H__ __ t__ __ y
4 C__ __ __ __ i__ __ __ __ y
5 F__ __ __ __ __ __ g__ L__ __ g__ __ g__ __
6 P__ __ s__ c__
7 C__ __ __ p__ __ __ __ r S__ __ __ __ n__ e
8 M__ __ __ __ s
9 A__ __ __
10 M__ __ __ __ c
11 D__ __ __ __ __ a
12 G__ __ __ g__ __ __ __ y

2 ⭐⭐ Complete the timetable with the school subjects from Exercise 1.

MONDAY

9.00 a.m. – 9.50 a.m. ¹*Art*
(painting)

9.50 a.m. – 10.30 a.m. ²_____
(how plants grow)

10.30 a.m. – 10.50 a.m. Break

10.50 a.m. – 11.30 a.m. ³_____ _____
(football / tennis)

11.30 a.m. – 12.10 p.m. ⁴_____
(Romeo and Juliet; I'm Romeo!)

12.10 p.m. – 1.50 p.m. Lunch

1.50 p.m. – 2.30 p.m. ⁵_____
(atoms and electricity)

2.30 p.m. – 3.10 p.m. ⁶_____
(Beethoven's 9th symphony on piano)

TUESDAY

9.00 a.m. – 9.50 a.m. ⁷_____ _____
(French)

9.50 a.m. – 10.30 a.m. ⁸_____
(Queen Victoria 1837–1901)

10.30 a.m. – 10.50 a.m. Break

10.50 a.m. – 11.30 a.m. ⁹_____
(10% of 124)

11.30 a.m. – 12.10 p.m. ¹⁰_____
(countries of South America)

12.10 p.m. – 1.50 p.m. Lunch

1.50 p.m. – 2.30 p.m. ¹¹_____
(writing a computer programme)

2.30 p.m. – 3.10 p.m. ¹²_____
(H_2O and other elements)

3 ⭐⭐ Complete the questions with the words from the box. There are two extra words.

calculator dictionary folder headphones
highlighter keys ruler school backpack textbooks
~~tissue~~

1 I need to clean my face. Have you got a *tissue*?
2 I can't work out 24 x 56 in my head. Can I use your _____?
3 Your bag is full of important pieces of paper. Why don't you keep them tidy in a _____?
4 I don't know this word. Can I borrow your _____?
5 Don't leave your books on the table. Why don't you put them in the _____?
6 Those lines are not very straight. Why don't you use a _____?
7 I want you to do Exercise 3 on page 75. Can you open your _____, please?
8 I want to remember these words. Can I borrow your yellow _____?

4 ⭐⭐ Complete the dialogue with the words from the box.

calculator dictionary Foreign headphones ~~key~~
Maths notebook ruler

Miranda Oh, no!
Callum What's wrong?
Miranda I haven't got the ¹*key* for my locker.
Callum What's inside it?
Miranda My Maths textbook. I need that. It's got all the homework exercises in it.
Callum You can look at Beth's and write them in your ²_____.
Miranda That's in the locker too.
Callum Oh.
Miranda And my English-French ³_____. I need it to translate these words for this afternoon. I'm terrible at ⁴_____ Languages. And my highlighters.
Callum What do you need them for?
Miranda To highlight new words so I can learn them. My ⁵_____ is in there too.
Callum Is that important?
Miranda Yes. I like to draw lines under the name of the topic. And I haven't got a ⁶_____.
Callum Use the one on your phone.
Miranda We can't use phones in ⁷_____ lessons. What a terrible day!
Callum Don't worry! It isn't important. Relax. Oh, by the way. Can I have my ⁸_____? I want to listen to music on the bus home.
Miranda Sorry, Callum :(. They're in the locker too.

5 ON A HIGH NOTE Write about the most important things you need to take to school. Explain why they are important and for which lessons.

UNIT VOCABULARY PRACTICE > page 49

4C GRAMMAR

Present Simple and Present Continuous

1 ★ Complete the sentences with the correct forms in bold.

GO / AM GOING

1 I usually _go_ to school by car. Today, I _am going_ by bus.

PLAY FOOTBALL / ARE RUNNING

2 In today's PE lesson, we _____, but we usually _____.

READS / ISN'T READING

3 My sister _____ a book at the moment. It isn't surprising. She never _____ books.

WATCH / ARE WATCHING

4 My parents hardly ever _____ TV. They _____ TV today because there is some very important news.

TALK / ARE TALKING

5 My friends and I _____ about Cathy's new haircut. We usually _____ about school work or our plans for the weekend, but Cathy's hair is amazing!

DOESN'T COME / ISN'T COMING

6 Our teacher _____ usually _____ to lessons late. Where is he? Oh, wait, here is another teacher. Our teacher _____ today so she is here to teach us instead.

2 ★ Match questions 1–8 with short answers a–h.

1 ☐ Are you wearing jeans today?

2 ☐ Is you sister eating breakfast at the moment?

3 ☐ Does your brother listen to music?

4 ☐ Do your parents work at the weekend?

5 ☐ Is your brother listening to music now?

6 ☐ Do you wear a uniform to school?

7 ☐ Are your parents working at the moment?

8 ☐ Does your sister always eat breakfast?

a Yes, he does.

b Yes, they are.

c Yes, I am.

d Yes, she does.

e No, I don't.

f No, they don't.

g No, she isn't.

h No, he isn't.

3 ★★ USE OF ENGLISH Choose the correct words a–c to complete the text.

NON-UNIFORM DAY

At our school, we usually wear a uniform but **1**__ a year, we have a non-uniform day. It's the non-uniform day today! Hooray!

Every year, someone forgets about the non-uniform day. This year, it's Marta. She's wearing her school uniform. She isn't very happy! Three girls **2**__ all wearing the same clothes. At the **3**__ some students from Year 8 are taking photos of them.

The teachers **4**__ usually wear a uniform but they wear nice clothes. Today they are wearing their normal clothes! Boring! They **5**__ join in with the non-uniform day. I don't know why not.

One last thing. The non-uniform day is not a non-work day, but we don't **6**__ do much work. Now we are in our French class. The teacher **7**__ for a video to show us – but she can't find it. She isn't in the classroom so we **8**__!

1	**a** one	**b** once	**c** every
2	**a** are	**b** is	**c** do
3	**a** now	**b** moment	**c** time
4	**a** aren't	**b** don't	**c** doesn't
5	**a** aren't	**b** isn't	**c** never
6	**a** often	**b** never	**c** now
7	**a** looks	**b** is looking	**c** look
8	**a** are relaxing	**b** relax	**c** relaxes

4 ★★★ Read the answers and write questions in the Present Simple or the Present Continuous.

1 _Where does your teacher live?_
My teacher lives in Dartford.

2 _____?
My dad is sleeping at the moment.

3 _____?
I usually go to bed at eleven o'clock.

4 _____?
My mum is wearing jeans and a T-shirt.

5 _____?
Today I am sitting next to Jason.

6 _____?
I usually sit next to Mark but he isn't here today.

7 _____?
I play sports about three times a week.

8 _____?
I'm reading a book called _American Panda_.

5 ON A HIGH NOTE Imagine you are doing something unusual today. Write about your normal day and what you are doing today which is different.

4D READING AND VOCABULARY

1 Read the text quickly and complete the notes.

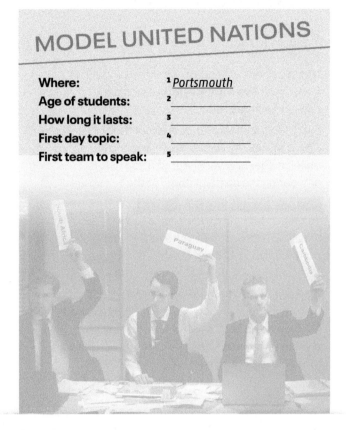

MODEL UNITED NATIONS

Where:	¹ *Portsmouth*
Age of students:	² _____
How long it lasts:	³ _____
First day topic:	⁴ _____
First team to speak:	⁵ _____

2 Read the text again and answer the questions.

1 Where are the students at the Model United Nations event from?
from all over Europe

2 What kind of subjects do they study?
_____

3 How long do the teams have to do their research?
_____

4 How many teams does the writer mention?
_____

5 Is everybody in the writer's team happy with their presentation?
_____

Vocabulary extension

3 Match the highlighted words from the text with the definitions.

1 The study of governments and power. *Politics*

2 People whom a group or country chooses to represent them. _____

3 A talk to a group of people, often with pictures, films, music or other forms of multimedia. _____

4 People who are at school with you. _____

5 The study of a topic in order to discover new facts.
_____

6 Something you get for winning a competition or doing good work. _____

7 A talk between two or more people who give their ideas or opinions on a topic. _____

4 Complete the sentences with the correct forms of the words from Exercise 3.

1 I'm now friends on Facebook with all my *schoolmates* – even the ones I don't like very much!

2 At the moment, in History we're having a _____ about life in the 19th century.

3 Some students are giving a _____ about their favourite kinds of music. It's really interesting.

4 My parents are very interested in _____. They always watch the news and vote in elections.

5 Every year we choose two student _____ to go to meetings with the teachers.

6 The _____ for the winners of the Spanish competition is a free term at a local language school.

7 When we do projects at school, we go to the computer room to do _____ about the topic first.

ACTIVE VOCABULARY | Negative prefix *un-*

We often use the prefix *-un* to make adjectives negative (e.g. *usual - **un**usual*).

---

5 Complete the sentences with the negative forms of the adjectives from the box.

able ~~clear~~ friendly happy lucky

1 The meaning of this word is still *unclear* to me. Can you explain it again, please?

2 Our new neighbour is rather _____. He hardly ever says hello when we meet him.

3 We are _____ to do this test because it's too difficult for us.

4 Lisa is always _____. She often buys lottery tickets but never wins anything.

5 Why are you _____ today? Is something wrong?

6 **ON A HIGH NOTE** What meetings or special events happen at your school? Think of one and write a short 'live blog' describing what people are doing and how they are feeling.

UNIT VOCABULARY PRACTICE > page 49

Model United Nations

Hi, today I'm at a Model United Nations event here in Portsmouth. There are students from all over Europe here. They're discussing politics and solving problems. It's a kind of role-play where students play the part of delegates to the UN.

10.30 a.m. The students here are all between 16 and 18 years old. Some study Politics or Economics at school, others do typical subjects such as Maths or Sciences. Some people say we're only here because we get three days off school, but that's unfair. We're reading, writing and sharing ideas. The days are long. This isn't an easy option.
This is the first of three days and while my schoolmates are taking part in the activities, I'm here to explain what is going on and why. First of all, each group plays the part of a country. My team is Norway. Today we're discussing global warming and what each country is doing to help the problem. We have three hours to do research in the mornings and then, after lunch every day, each country gives a presentation. Everyone is very nervous and working hard. Our desk is very untidy and full of pieces of paper.

14.00 p.m. It's the afternoon now. The Turkish team is the first to speak. They are talking about the problem in their country and telling us about their plans for the future. Other students are busy taking notes. It's Canada next and then Norway! We are unlucky because the Canadian team is really good.

14.30 p.m. It's our turn. James, one of our delegates, is very nervous. He looks unwell! I hope he's OK.

17.00 p.m. The discussion is over. We're taking a break now. The students in our team are discussing their presentation. Some people are happy, but some aren't. Some of their comments to other team members are a bit unkind but it's just because they want to do well. There are prizes for the best delegates at the end of the three days. For some people, it isn't important to win or lose but others care a lot! They're the ones who are unhappy.

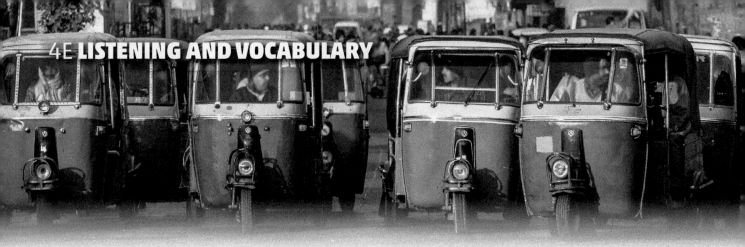

1 🔊 **23** Listen to a conversation and decide if statements 1–3 are true or false.

   1 ☐ Oliver goes to an international school in India.

   2 ☐ Oliver knows Bella from his old school in Britain.

   3 ☐ Bella invites Oliver to visit his old school in the evening.

2 🔊 **23** Listen to the conversation again and choose the correct answers.

   1 Oliver says that

     a all his lessons are in English.

     b all the international schools in Delhi are English speaking schools.

     c all his teachers come from Great Britain.

   2 Which of these sentences about Oliver's school is true?

     a There are no Indian students there.

     b The students are all either Indian or English.

     c There are more Indian students than English students.

   3 Oliver likes his classmates because

     a he has a lot of English friends.

     b he can find out new information from them.

     c they are all very similar.

   4 From what Bella and Oliver say, we know that

     a Oliver doesn't know any people going to the café.

     b Oliver doesn't need much money for the visit to the café.

     c Oliver is sure that he can go to the café.

Vocabulary extension

3 🔊 **24** Complete the extracts from the recording in Exercise 1 with the words from the box. Listen and check.

believe   imagine   let   ~~miss~~   seems

   1 I *miss* home sometimes but I love the people, the food, the weather!

   2 'Sometimes it _____ quite strange to be in an English classroom with English teachers but, outside, it's India.' 'I can _____!'

   3 You may not _____ it but, there is only one other English person.

   4 Can I _____ you know later?

4 ON A HIGH NOTE Write about some good and bad things about your school.

Pronunciation

> ### ACTIVE PRONUNCIATION | /iː/ sound
>
> In English, /iː/ is a long vowel sound (e.g. *tree*).
> We can spell /iː/ in different ways:
> • ee (e.g. *see*)
> • ea (e.g. *leave*)
> • ey (e.g. *key*)

5 🔊 **25** Listen to the /iː/ sound on its own and in different words and repeat.

6 🔊 **26** Listen and write seven words which have the /iː/ sound.

   1 *see*

   2 _____

   3 _____

   4 _____

   5 _____

   6 _____

   7 _____

7 Complete the table with the words from Exercise 6.

/iː/ sound spelled with *ee*	/iː/ sound spelled with *ea*
see	

8 🔊 **27** All the words below have the /iː/ sound. Complete the words with the letters *ea* or *ee*. Listen and repeat.

   1 m*ea*l   **5** agr__ __

   2 b__ __f   **6** cl__ __n

   3 dr__ __m   **7** ch__ __se

   4 t__ __nager   **8** r__ __d

9 🔊 **28** Complete the sentences with one word in each gap. Each word has the /iː/ sound. Listen and check.

   1 I play football for the school *team*.

   2 Put the ice _____ in the freezer to keep it cold.

   3 Do you prefer swimming in a pool or in the _____?

   4 How much sugar is in this coffee? It's really _____.

   5 I'm really tired. I need to _____.

UNIT VOCABULARY PRACTICE > page 49

1 🔊 *29* **Listen and repeat the phrases. How do you say them in your language?**

SPEAKING | Asking for, giving and refusing permission

ASKING FOR PERMISSION

Can I borrow your headphones, **please?**

Could I borrow your calculator?

Is it OK if I use your ruler?

SAYING 'YES'

Yes, of course.

Yes, sure. Here you are.

Yes, that's fine.

That's no problem.

SAYING 'NO' (AND GIVING A REASON)

No, sorry. I don't have one.

I'm sorry but you can't. I'm using it at the moment.

---

2 **Complete the mini-conversations with one word in each gap.**

Adam	Can I borrow your dictionary, please?
Bill	Yes, **1** *sure*.
Jane	Can I borrow 50p for the bus?
Suzie	Yes, that's no **2** p_____.
Ahmed	Can I use your calculator, please?
Lucy	No, **3** s_____. I don't have one.
Mark	Is it OK if I sit here?
Patrick	Yes, of **4** c_____.
Frank	Could I borrow your pen, **5** p_____?
Sam	I'm sorry, but you can't. I'm using it at the moment.
Brendon	Could I use your phone to call my mum?
James	Yes, that's **6** f_____.
Emily	Could I borrow your highlighter, please?
Kelly	Yes, **7** h_____ you are.

3 **Choose the correct words to complete the sentences.**

1 I'm sorry *but / and* you can't at the moment.

2 Is it OK *that / if* I use your ruler?

3 Can I use your calculator? This *one / ones* doesn't work.

4 I'm sorry. *I use / I'm using* my pen at the moment.

5 Use my dictionary. The *one / ones* on the shelf are really old and some of the pages are missing.

6 I have a lot of papers on my desk. Could *I / you* borrow this folder to sort them?

4 **Read the questions and write answers using the words in brackets.**

Can I use your ruler?

1 *No, sorry. I don't have one.* ✗ (have)

2 _____ ✓ (fine)

3 _____ ✓ (problem)

Can I borrow your pen?

4 _____ ✓ (course)

5 _____ ✗ (using)

6 _____ ✓ (here)

5 🔊 *30* **Complete the dialogue with one word in each gap. Listen and check.**

Nina	Hi. **1** *Can* I sit here?
Jessica	**2** _____, that's fine. Are you a new student?
Nina	Yes. My name's Nina.
Jessica	Hi, Nina. I'm Jessica.
Nina	Hi, Jessica. **3** _____ it OK **4** _____ I look at your notebook?
Jessica	Yes, that's no **5** _____. Here you **6** _____.
Nina	Thanks. Wow. This French is really difficult. Can I borrow your dictionary?
Jessica	Sorry. This is my Spanish dictionary. I haven't got my French **7** _____ with me.
Nina	Oh. Can you tell me what this word means?
Jessica	Yes, of **8** _____. It means …

We're asking you about your ideal school day. Here are some of your ideas.

My name's Colleen Ramsey. I'm 15 and I'm in year ten of school.

My ideal school day starts at 9.30 (not like my normal school day which starts at 9.00) so I get an extra half an hour in bed. The day starts with an Art lesson. The teacher talks about a famous painter or style of art and then <u>we</u> paint a picture in that style. The teacher is very kind, and <u>she</u> always tells us that <u>our</u> paintings are great!

After Art we have English but on my ideal day, we don't learn grammar. We read novels and talk about <u>them</u> in the class. Sometimes we write short stories. I love writing. Then we have Spanish with a young teacher from Spain or South America. We speak a lot in the lessons and listen to Spanish songs. <u>They</u>'re cool. And on my ideal school day I understand all the words I hear!

Lunch on my ideal school day is pizza. We sit in the canteen and the local pizza restaurant brings us our favourite pizza. Mine is Hawaiian pizza with sweet corn and pineapple. After lunch we have PE. We go to the school pool. We have a two-hour swimming lesson <u>there</u>. School finishes at 3 p.m. and, of course, we don't have any homework!

Unfortunately, I never have an ideal school day!

- Introduce yourself.
- Describe when the day starts and what happens in the morning.
- Describe what happens at lunchtime.
- Describe the afternoon and after-school activities.

1 **Complete the sentences about Colleen and yourself.**

1 Colleen is *fifteen* years old. I am _____.

2 Colleen's ideal day starts with _____. My ideal day starts with _____.

3 On Colleen's ideal day, she writes _____ in English. In my ideal English lesson, we _____.

4 Colleen learns _____ as a foreign language. On my ideal school day, I study _____ as a foreign language.

5 On Colleen's ideal school day, she eats _____ for lunch. On my ideal school day, I eat _____ for lunch.

6 In the afternoon, on Colleen's ideal school day, she has _____. On my ideal school day, in the afternoon, I _____.

2 **Look at the underlined words in the text and write what they refer to.**

1 we   *students*

2 she   _____

3 our   _____

4 them   _____

5 they   _____

6 there   _____

3 **Rewrite the text. Replace the underlined parts with pronouns or *one/ones* to avoid repeating nouns.**

There are a lot of clubs in the afternoon at my school. My friends and I go to a film club. <u>My friends and I</u> are really interested in watching and making films. Our English teacher, Miss Logan, organises the film club. <u>Miss Logan</u> always shows us about 20 minutes of a famous film. Then we talk about <u>the film</u>. Sometimes we give presentations about our favourite films. I'm preparing <u>a presentation</u> at the moment. <u>The presentation</u> is about my favourite film: *The Sun is also a Star*. I like the films my friends talk about, but the <u>films</u> Miss Logan chooses are more interesting because I don't know them.

There are a lot of clubs in the afternoon at my school. My friends and I go to a film club. We are really interested in watching and making films.

_____

_____

_____

_____

_____

_____

4 WRITING TASK **Write about an after-school club you enjoy.**

ACTIVE WRITING | An Internet forum post

1 **Plan your post.**

- Think about the after-school clubs you go to. If you don't go to any, use your imagination.
- Make notes about the day and time the club takes place and what you do there.
- Think about what you like and dislike about the club.

2 **Write the post.**

- Start with a sentence about yourself and the club you are going to write about.
- Use three or four paragraphs to organise your post.
- Use the Present Simple and adverbs of frequency to talk about what you do at the club.
- Use the Present Continuous to talk about anything you are doing at the moment at the club.
- Use pronouns and the words *one/ones* to avoid repeating nouns.

3 **Check that ...**

- you have included all the relevant information.
- there are no spelling or grammar mistakes.

1 **4A GRAMMAR AND VOCABULARY Match the words from the box with their definitions.**

~~canteen~~ gym library playing fields science lab staff room

1 This is where we eat our lunch. *canteen*

2 We play football here. _____

3 We get books from here. _____

4 You can find the teachers here when they aren't teaching. _____

5 We go here for Chemistry lessons and do experiments. _____

6 We have PE here when it's raining. _____

2 **4B VOCABULARY Complete the words with one letter in each gap.**

MONDAY

8.00: ¹B*iology*
Plants and animals

8.45: ²P__y_____s
Magnetism

9.30: ³A_____
Painting

10.15: ⁴G_____g_____h__
Countries and continents

11.00: Computer ⁵S_____e_____e
Writing computer code

11.45: Maths
Don't forget ⁶c_____c__l_____r.

13.30: ⁷F__r_____g__ Languages:
French in room 5, Spanish in room 8
Bring a bilingual ⁸d_____t_____n_____y.

14.15: ⁹D_____a
Acting in a short play

15.00: ¹⁰P_____s_____l E____c_____n
Today in the gym

Don't forget:
¹¹t__xtb_____s, notebooks and a ¹²f_____d__r for any pieces of paper the teachers give us.

3 **4D READING AND VOCABULARY Choose the correct words to complete the sentences.**

1 At the moment, in History, we are __ a project.
   a taking   **b** getting   **c** doing

2 We need 50% or more to __ this exam.
   a pass   **b** fail   **c** get

3 I usually __ good grades – As or Bs.
   a get   **b** pass   **c** take

4 I like __ exams. I just don't like getting my results.
   a making   **b** working   **c** taking

5 In this school, we __ a lot of interesting subjects like Art and Dance.
   a work   **b** do   **c** make

6 I really don't want to __ this exam.
   a pass   **b** manage   **c** fail

7 Well done! The exam is over. Now you can __ a break.
   a make   **b** take   **c** get

8 It's important to __ a lot of qualifications.
   a pass   **b** get   **c** take

4 **4E LISTENING AND VOCABULARY Complete the text with the words from the box.**

crowded dangerous expensive freezing ~~simple~~ tiny

REAL HOLIDAY EXPERIENCE

There's a holiday advert on the television. Two people are getting on a plane. They're happy and relaxed. When they get off, it's a beautiful day and they get into a car and drive to a small village near the sea. The beach is quiet, the people are friendly and the food is ¹*simple* but delicious. After a day on the beach, they drive to a town. All the cool people go there because the restaurants and cafés are great, and bands play concerts outside in the evening.

The problem is that real life isn't like that. When you go on holiday, the airport is ²_____ with people. When you get to your hotel, it's old and your room is ³_____. There isn't even anywhere to put your bag. The room is also ⁴_____ because there is no heating. You want to eat but the only food you can buy is from a burger bar because the local restaurants are really ⁵_____ and you haven't got much money! There's a nice beach but it's difficult to get to it because there's a busy road and it's ⁶_____ to cross it!

5 **ON A HIGH NOTE Choose a school subject and say what happens in a typical lesson. Write what you are studying in that subject at the moment.**

1 **For each learning objective, write 1–5 to assess your ability.**

1 = I don't feel confident. 5 = I feel confident.

	Learning objective	Course material	How confident I am (1–5)
4A	I can use the Present Continuous to talk about things happening now or temporary situations.	Student's Book pp. 50–51 Workbook pp. 40–41	
4B	I can talk about school, school subjects and classroom objects.	Student's Book p. 52 Workbook p. 42	
4C	I can use the Present Simple and the Present Continuous to talk about regular actions and activities happening now.	Student's Book p. 53 Workbook p. 43	
4D	I can identify specific information in an article and talk about school life.	Student's Book pp. 54–55 Workbook pp. 44–45	
4E	I can identify key details in a podcast and talk about commuting.	Student's Book p. 56 Workbook p. 46	
4F	I can ask for and give or refuse permission.	Student's Book p. 57 Workbook p. 47	
4G	I can describe a typical day at my school.	Student's Book p. 58 Workbook p. 48	

2 **Which of the skills above would you like to improve in? How?**

Skill I want to improve in	How I can improve

3 **What can you remember from this unit?**

New words I learned and most want to remember	Expressions and phrases I liked	English I heard or read outside class

Self-check

GRAMMAR AND VOCABULARY

1 Choose the correct words to complete the sentences.

1 Chemistry and Art are both ___.
   a languages   **b** subjects   **c** objects
2 We study plants and animals in ___.
   a Physics   **b** Biology   **c** Chemistry
3 You can carry your school books in a ___.
   a folder   **b** highlighter   **c** school backpack
4 You need a ___ to draw straight lines.
   a calculator   **b** ruler   **c** key
5 You can pass or fail ___.
   a a grade   **b** an exam   **c** a qualification

   / 5

2 Complete the sentences with the correct words formed from the words in bold.

1 When the temperature goes below 0°C, we say that it's *freezing*. **FREEZE**
2 Chemistry lessons can be _____ so listen to what your teacher tells you. **DANGER**
3 What _____ do you need to become a doctor? **QUALIFY**
4 Can we use a _____ in our Maths exam? **CALCULATE**
5 PE is short for Physical _____. **EDUCATE**
6 When it's sunny, we do PE on the school _____ fields. **PLAY**

   / 5

3 Use the prompts to write questions in the Present Simple or the Present Continuous.

1 **a** What / you / usually / do / in your free time?
   What do you usually do in your free time?
   b What / you / do / at the moment?
   _____

2 **a** Who / Lisa / usually / sit / next to in Maths?
   _____
   b Who / she / sit / next to today?
   _____

3 **a** What / your teacher / wear / today?
   _____
   b she / always / wear the same clothes?
   _____

   / 5

4 Complete the text with the correct Present Simple or Present Continuous forms of the verbs in brackets.

Some French students are at our school this week. They ¹*are learning* (learn) English in an English school. It's a great idea and it ² _____ (happen) every year. One of the students ³ _____ (stay) at our house. My parents ⁴ _____ (not speak) French so she ⁵ _____ (speak) to them in English all the time. Her English ⁶ _____ (get) better every day. It's a great way to learn a language. I hope I can spend a week in France one day!

   / 5

USE OF ENGLISH

5 Choose the correct words a–c to complete the texts.

1
> Basketball practice today in the ___. 15.45–16.45. Everyone welcome.

   a canteen   **b** gym   **c** lab

2
> Year 12 students are ___ an exam. Please be quiet.

   a making   **b** getting   **c** taking

3
> If you lose the ___ to your locker, please tell your teacher immediately.

   a key   **b** desk   **c** ruler

4
> All Year 10 students, please ___ the new timetable – there are some changes.

   a do   **b** make   **c** check

5
> Students can borrow two books for one week from the ___. Please do not lose them.

   a library   **b** staff room   **c** hallway

   / 5

6 Complete the text with one word in each gap.

Dear Parents,

As you know, we organise several trips for students each year, ¹*for* example to banks, transport companies and local newspapers. ² _____ the moment, the Year 10 Computer Science students ³ _____ learning about computer code and how to write ⁴ _____. To help them, we're organising a visit to a local computing company.

The company is only 2 km from the school, so I think the students and teachers can go ⁵ _____ foot. Mr Paine, the Computer Science teacher is organising the visit. Please contact ⁶ _____ with any questions you have.

Thank you,

Elaine Simpson

Headmistress

   / 5
   / 30

51

05 Appearances

5A GRAMMAR AND VOCABULARY

Past Simple: *to be* and *can*

1 ⭐ **Choose the correct forms to complete the sentences.**

1 Yesterday *was / were* a really bad day.
2 Where *was / were* you last night?
3 The students *was / were* noisy and the teacher *was / were* angry.
4 David Bowie *was / were* my dad's favourite singer.
5 My parents met when they *was / were* at university.
6 When we *was / were* in Slovakia, our apartment *was / were* in a street called John Lennon Street.
7 My dad *was / were* late home last night and we *was / were* worried.

2 ⭐ **Match questions 1–7 with short answers a–g.**

1 ☐ Were you late for school this morning?
2 ☐ Was Madonna in a James Bond film?
3 ☐ Could Picasso and Van Gogh paint?
4 ☐ Could your grandmother sing?
5 ☐ Were Ryan Gosling and Emma Stone married in the film *La La Land*?
6 ☐ Was I there when it happened?
7 ☐ Could George Clooney play baseball when he was young?

a No, she couldn't.
b Yes, he could.
c No, I wasn't.
d Yes, you were.
e Yes, she was.
f No, they weren't.
g Yes, they could.

3 ⭐⭐ **Complete the text with *was*, *were*, *wasn't*, *weren't*, *could* or *couldn't*.**

When I was young, I **1** *couldn't* read well. It **2** _____ very difficult for me. At school, all the other children **3** _____ read well but not me. My parents **4** _____ very worried. Then, one day, I watched a TV show called *Hank Zipzer*. It was about a boy like me. The writer, Henry Winkler, had the same problems that I had. He **5** _____ read well at school, either. My parents bought me the first Hank Zipzer book. It **6** _____ easy to read, but I wanted to finish it and, in the end, I did.

The books **7** _____ easy to find in our town but I eventually got them all. My reading got better, and I still often read them these days.

Past Simple: affirmative

4 ⭐ **Which verbs are regular and which are irregular? Find the odd one out in each group.**

1 ask (do) live start
2 describe die have remain
3 refuse study talk win
4 be can come watch
5 get give go like
6 eat love speak teach

5 ⭐⭐ **Complete the sentences with *last*, *ago* or *in*.**

1 I was at a concert *last* week.
2 My mum taught English four years _____.
3 We ate pizza _____ Thursday.
4 Paul started boxing _____ 2018.
5 My parents came here half an hour _____.
6 We lived in London _____ year.

6 ⭐⭐ **Put the words in order to make sentences.**

1 year / studied / last / we / the Past Simple
We studied the Past Simple last year.

2 2017 / friends / in / my / visited / China
_____

3 week / we / exam / last / an / had
_____

4 an / ago / watched / days / old / two / Tom / film
_____

5 in / job / 2016 / got / new / mum / a / my
_____

7 ★★ Complete the text with the correct Past Simple forms of the verbs in brackets.

There's a famous photo of a pretty woman wearing sunglasses and looking into a shop window. The woman is Audrey Hepburn. She **1** _was_ (be) born in Belgium in 1929 but **2**_____ (move) to England when she was a young girl. In 1940, she and her mother **3**_____ (be) on holiday in Holland when the German army **4**_____ (arrive). They **5**_____ (not can) leave and **6**_____ (spend) the war there. It **7**_____ (be) a difficult time for Audrey.

After the war, she **8**_____ (start) acting and **9**_____ (go) to Hollywood in 1951. Two years later, she **10**_____ (win) an Oscar for the film *Roman Holiday*.

Later in her life, she **11**_____ (become) a UN ambassador. Sadly, she **12**_____ (die) at the age of 63 but she is still famous and a big influence on many people.

8 ★★ Use the prompts to write sentences in the Past Simple.

1 last Saturday: I / have / a party
2 2017: Miss Lewis / start / teaching
3 2 weeks ago: dad / get / new job
4 last month: sister / win / an English competition
5 2015: mum / be / an anti-war protester
6 3 months ago: our class / go / on a school trip
7 10 years ago: I / not / can / speak French
8 2004: sister / be / born

1 *I had a party last Saturday.*
2 _____
3 _____
4 _____
5 _____
6 _____
7 _____
8 _____

9 ★★★ Complete the text with the correct Past Simple forms of the verbs from the box.

call die do have ~~help~~ love talk try work
write

The First Lady of the United States is a title we give to the President's wife. (When there is a woman President, we can have the first 'First Man'.)

Many first ladies become very popular. Michelle Obama **1**helped her husband to become president in 2009. When he was President, Michelle **2**_____ very hard as well. She **3**_____ to improve education and health care. She also **4**_____ to people about healthy food and doing more physical activity. People **5**_____ Michelle Obama!

Eleanor Roosevelt was First Lady from 1933 to 1945. She **6**_____ a lot to help human rights. She **7**_____ newspaper articles and she **8**_____ her own radio show. When her husband **9**_____ in 1945, the new President, Harry Truman **10**_____ Eleanor Roosevelt 'The First Lady of the World'.

10 ON A HIGH NOTE Write a few sentences about an inspiring person you know.

5B VOCABULARY | Appearance, clothes

1 ★ **Put the words from the box under the correct headings.**

~~boots~~ cardigan gloves hat hoody scarf shoes
skirt top tracksuit bottoms trainers trousers T-shirt

1 What you wear on your feet:

   boots

   _____

   _____

2 What you wear on your legs:

   _____

   _____

   _____

3 What you wear on your body:

   _____

   _____

   _____

   _____

4 What you wear when it's cold outside:

   _____

   _____

   _____

2 ★★ **Write the names of clothes that match these definitions.**

1 They are trousers. They are often blue. j_eans_

2 Women wear this on their body and legs. d_____

3 It's like a small coat. You wear it when it isn't very cold or rainy. j_____

4 Men usually wear one to work under a suit. s_____

5 You wear these on your feet under your shoes. They keep your feet warm. s_____

6 You usually wear this on top of your T-shirt and under your coat to keep warm. j_____

7 It's longer than a jacket. You wear it when it's cold or rainy. c_____

3 ★★ **Complete the dialogue with one word in each gap.**

Val Tell me about your new teacher.

Josh What about him?

Val Is he old?

Josh He isn't old, and he isn't young. He's **1**m_iddle_-a_ged_.

Val Is he tall?

Josh No, he's quite **2**s_____.

Val Is he well-built?

Josh Not really. He is quite **3**s_____, not too thin and definitely not fat. He's quite **4**g_____-l_____. He's got a nice **5**s_____.

Val Oh, is that him?

Josh No, that person has got long, dark, **6**w_____ hair. Our new teacher is **7**b_____ – no hair at all!

Val Really? What colour are his eyes?

Josh I don't know. I know he's got a big, black **8**b_____, though.

4 ★★★ **Put the words in order to make sentences.**

1 new / jumper / my / blue / where's / ?
   Where's my new, blue jumper?

2 long / lovely / like / hair / have / blonde / I'd / to

   _____

3 this / long / T-shirt / love / red / funny / I

   _____

4 a / got / uniform / grey / terrible / school / we've

   _____

5 eyes / very / red / got / tired / you've

   _____

6 running / buy / I / white / shoes / can / cheap / these / ?

   _____

5 ON A HIGH NOTE **Describe someone in your family. Write about their appearance and the clothes they usually wear.**

UNIT VOCABULARY PRACTICE > page 61

5C SPEAKING

1 🔊 **31 Listen and repeat the phrases. How do you say them in your language?**

SPEAKING | Shopping for clothes

WHAT SALES ASSISTANTS SAY

Can I help you?

Do you need any help?

What size are you?

The changing rooms are over there.

Does it/Do they fit?

WHAT CUSTOMERS SAY

Yes, please. I'm looking for a jacket.

No, thanks. I'm just looking.

Small/Medium/Large

Can I try this/these on?

Yes, it's/they're perfect.

Have you got this T-shirt in a small?

Have you got this shirt in a medium?

Have you got this jumper in a large?

Does it/Do they suit me?

No, it doesn't look right.

---

2 Who says these questions? Write *SA* for the sales assistant or *C* for the customer.

1 What size are you? _SA_

2 Hi. Can I help you? ___

3 Have you got this shirt in a medium? ___

4 Does it suit me? ___

5 Can I try them on? ___

3 Match answers a–e with questions 1–6 from Exercise 2.

a ☐ Yes, here you are.

b ☐ Of course. The changing rooms are over there.

c ☐ Medium, I think.

d ☐ No, thanks. I'm just looking.

e ☐ Yes, it's perfect.

4 Choose the correct responses to complete the mini-conversations.

1

Assistant   Can I help you?   **Customer** ___

a Yes, please. I'm looking for trainers.

b No, it doesn't look right.

c Yes, they're perfect.

2

Assistant   What size are you?   **Customer** ___

a I'm just looking.

b I really like it.

c Large, I think.

3

Customer   Can I try it on?   **Assistant** ___

a Yes, of course.

b What size are you?

c It's perfect.

4

Customer   Does it suit me?   **Assistant** ___

a No, thanks. I'm just looking.

b Yes, it's perfect.

c Of course. It's over there.

5 Complete the second sentence with two words so that it means the same as the first one.

1 Can I help you?

  Do you **_need any_** help?

2 Are they the right size?

  Do _____?

3 Do they look good on me?

  Do _____ me?

4 Are you small, medium or large?

  What _____ you?

5 Can I see what they look like on me?

  Can I _____ on?

6 🔊 **32 Complete the dialogue with one word in each gap. Listen and check.**

Assistant   Good afternoon. Do you **¹**_need_ any help?

Customer   Yes, please. I'm **²**_____ for a summer dress.

Assistant   What **³**_____ are you?

Customer   Small.

Assistant   This one is nice.

Customer   Have you got this **⁴**_____ red?

Assistant   Yes, **⁵**_____ you are.

Customer   Can I **⁶**_____ it on?

Assistant   Of course. The **⁷**_____ rooms are over there.

Later …

Customer   Does it **⁸**_____ me?

Assistant   Yes, it's perfect.

5D GRAMMAR

Past Simple: negative and question forms

1 ★ Read the questions and complete the short answers.

Sam Did you go to Belle's party last week?
Phil Yes, [1] _I did_.
Sam Did she have a good time?
Phil Yes, [2] _____.

Megan Did your parents take you to school yesterday?
Paul No, [3] _____.
Megan Did you go by bus?
Paul No, [4] _____. I walked.

Noah Did Simon ask Kylie on a date?
Lucy Yes, [5] _____.
Noah Did she say yes?
Lucy Yes, [6] _____.

Kerry Did I borrow a book from you last week?
Robert Yes, [7] _____.
Kerry Did I give it back to you yesterday?
Robert No, [8] _____.

2 ★ Choose the correct forms to complete the sentences.

1 I didn't *see / saw* my friends last Saturday.
2 Did you *go / went* out last night?
3 We didn't *have / had* French today because our teacher was ill.
4 I *get / got* a letter from my cousin yesterday.
5 When did Lisa and Frank *start / started* dating?
6 Mum *make / made* some cakes yesterday. They were great!
7 Where did you *buy / bought* your new jeans?

3 ★★ Match questions 1–6 with answers a–f. Then complete the answers with the correct Past Simple forms of the underlined verbs.

1 ☐ Who did you <u>meet</u> last night?
2 ☐ Where did you <u>go</u>?
3 ☐ What film did you <u>watch</u>?
4 ☐ What did you <u>talk</u> about?
5 ☐ Did you <u>have</u> anything to eat?
6 ☐ What time did you <u>get</u> home?

a We _____ about school, friends and teachers.
b I _____ Roberta.
c Yes, we _____ a pizza before the film.
d We _____ to the cinema.
e I think I _____ home just after 10 p.m.
f We _____ a film called *Shazam*.

4 ★★ Look at the information and correct the sentences.

> ### Last weekend
>
> Lee   visit grandparents
> Abigail   play tennis
> Zofia   do homework
> Marianna   meet friends
> Jack   sing in a concert
> Ben   go shopping
> Kelly   see a film at the cinema

Last weekend …

1 Lee went shopping.
   Lee didn't go shopping. He visited his grandparents.
2 Abigail visited her grandparents.
   _____
3 Zofia sang in a concert.
   _____
4 Marianna did her homework.
   _____
5 Jack met his friends.
   _____
6 Ben played tennis.
   _____
7 Kelly stayed at home.
   _____

5 ★★★ Read the answers and write *Wh-* questions.

1 _Who did you meet_ in the town centre?
   I met some friends from school.
2 When _____?
   I went to London yesterday.
3 Where _____?
   We travelled to France by car.
4 What time _____?
   I went to bed at 11 p.m. last night.
5 What _____?
   I ate chicken yesterday.
6 Why _____?
   I wore tracksuit bottoms to school yesterday because my trousers were dirty.
7 Why _____?
   We didn't get much homework today so I had time to hang out with friends.

6 ON A HIGH NOTE Write about things you did and didn't do last night/weekend/week.

1 🔊 33 Listen to Part 1 of an interview and answer the questions.

1 What's Tami's blog about?

_____

2 What item of clothing is she particularly interested in?

_____

3 Does she have a lot of shoes with high heels?

_____

2 🔊 34 Listen to Part 2 of the interview and complete the sentences with one or two words or a date.

1 Shoes with high heels originally came from _Persia_ in the fifteenth century.
2 They were worn by _____ riding on horses.
3 In Europe, only _____ could wear high-heels.
4 The French king, Louis XIV liked high heels because he was _____.
5 Men stopped wearing high heels in the _____ century.

Vocabulary extension

3 🔊 35 Complete the sentences with the words from the box, which you heard in the interview in Exercises 1 and 2. Listen and check.

collection ~~colourful~~ equal habits local practical

1 I like _colourful_ clothes, not boring black and grey ones.
2 This coat is very _____. It keeps me warm and dry, it's easy to wash, and it's light to carry.
3 'Do you have any bad _____?' 'I do. I never put my things away!'
4 We shouldn't think we are better than other people. All people are _____.
5 A _____ company made these shoes for me. Their shop is only 100 metres from my house.
6 Do you want to look at my _____ of comic books from around the world?

4 ON A HIGH NOTE Write about a fashion from the past that you like. Describe what people wore and why you like it.

Pronunciation

ACTIVE PRONUNCIATION | /s/ and /ʃ/ sounds

We usually use the letter _s_ in words with the sound /s/ (e.g. _size_) and the letters _sh_ in words with the sound /ʃ/ (e.g. **sh**oe).

Sometimes the spelling is different (e.g. /s/ – fa**c**e, **c**entre; /ʃ/ – edu**c**ation, ma**ch**ine, **s**ure).

5 🔊 36 Look at the groups of words. Circle in red the /s/ sounds and in green the /ʃ/ sounds. Listen and repeat.

1 gue**s**t	fa**sh**ion	intere**s**t
2 fir**s**t	hi**s**tory	**sh**oe
3 **s**oldier	hor**s**e	**s**o**c**iety
4 **s**oon	**s**ymbol	**sh**ort
5 **s**tarted	**sh**ow	**c**entury
6 **s**topped	le**ss**	awe**s**ome

6 🔊 37 Listen to ten words and write them in the correct column.

/s/ sound spelled with _s_	/s/ sound spelled with _c_
fast	

7 🔊 38 Listen to some words which contain the /ʃ/ sound and try to write them correctly.

1 _tradition_
2 _____
3 _____
4 _____
5 _____
6 _____
7 _____
8 _____
9 _____

8 🔊 39 When there are lots of /s/ and /ʃ/ sounds together they can be quite difficult to say. We call them tongue twisters in English. Listen and repeat this famous tongue twister.

She **s**ell**s** **s**ea **sh**ell**s** on the **s**ea **sh**ore.

9 🔊 40 Here are some more short tongue twisters. Listen and repeat them.

1 I'm wa**sh**ing the **sh**y **s**tudent's **sh**irt**s**.
2 Thi**s** i**s** the **ch**ef'**s** **s**peciality.
3 Let'**s** go **sh**opping for **s**ome **s**weet and **s**pi**c**y **s**auce.
4 Ta**s**te thi**s** fi**sh** di**sh**. It'**s** deliciou**s**.

5F READING AND VOCABULARY

1 **Read the text quickly and choose the best title.**

a An interesting year of research and discovery.

b Family tree websites compared and reviewed.

c Lost family photos turn up on family tree website.

2 **Read the text again. Match sentences A–F with gaps 1–4 in the text. There are two extra sentences.**

A However, it was fascinating to find out more about my family.

B That's why it took so long to find the information.

C So I decided to pay for one for a year.

D My grandmother looked like a film star.

E They were almost identical!

F Unfortunately, it is very difficult to go back further than that.

3 **Read the text again and answer the questions.**

1 What is the main difference between free websites and the ones you pay for?

Free websites don't have a lot of information.

2 What did the writer find in his parents' attic?

_____

3 Who was the woman who looked like his grandmother?

_____

4 What did the writer's great-uncle do for a living?

_____

5 How much time did the writer use the website for?

_____

Vocabulary extension

4 **Match the highlighted words from the text with the definitions.**

1 People who have a family connection to you. *relatives*

2 The event at which two people become husband and wife. _____

3 A diagram showing the relationship between people from different generations of a family. _____

4 Your grandfather's or grandmother's brother.

_____

5 Became husband and wife. _____

5 **Complete the sentences with the words from Exercise 4.**

1 My parents haven't got brothers or sisters, but I've got a *great-uncle* – my mother's father's brother.

2 I had a great time at my cousin's _____. I danced all evening!

3 We had a big family party for my grandfather's 70th birthday. Lots of _____ I didn't know came to the party.

4 My parents _____ in 1995 when they were 26 years old.

5 Our French teacher asked us to draw a _____ to practise family vocabulary in French.

ACTIVE VOCABULARY | Phrasal verbs

Phrasal verbs are made of a verb + a preposition or a verb + an adverb.

Sometimes the meaning is easy to understand from the words.

Take off *your shoes before you go into the house.*

Sometimes the meaning is completely different and not easy to understand.

*I felt excited when the plane **took off**.*

6 **Choose the correct words to complete the sentences. Use the text to help you if necessary.**

1 I came __ an interesting little shop on my way to the town centre last week.

a across   b off   c round

2 We had thirty minutes to do the test. I ran __ of time before I finished the last question.

a away   b up   c out

3 Schoolwork takes __ a lot of my time, so I don't go out during the week.

a out   b up   c in

4 I'd like to go __ to the 1960's to see what life was really like at that time.

a away   b along   c back

5 We live in London now, but my parents grew __ in a small town in the north of England.

a up   b off   c out

7 **Complete the sentences with the correct forms of the phrasal verbs from Exercise 6.**

1 Last night I was on my computer. I wanted to find a website that my friend told me about but then I *came across* a really interesting blog about fashion.

2 Last weekend I _____ of money and couldn't go to the cinema with my friends.

3 I'd like to _____ in time to see what my parents were like in school!

4 This is a good town to _____ in. It's safe, the schools are good and there's a lot to do here.

5 My friend loves having a horse but riding _____ a lot of her time.

8 **ON A HIGH NOTE Write about one of your ancestors. Describe what they did, where they lived and what they looked like.**

UNIT VOCABULARY PRACTICE > page 61

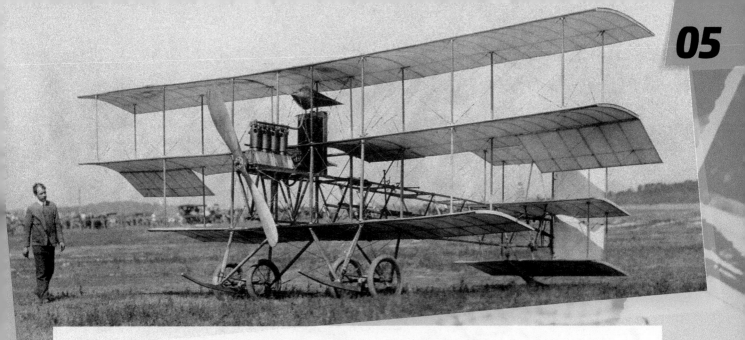

Last year, I decided to research my family tree and find out a little about my family background. Thanks to the Internet, you can get a lot of information online. Let me tell you what I did and what I discovered.

I started by looking at some of the many family tree websites. Some of them are free but most of them charge a fee. At first, I looked at the free sites, but I soon realised that there is a reason why they are free – they don't have a lot of information. **1**__ It was quite expensive, but definitely worth it.

I started by finding the relatives that I knew about. Slowly my research took me back to my great grandparents' parents who got married in 1880. **2**__ I tried but there was almost no information from the first half of the nineteenth century. So, instead, I decided to concentrate on my parents' and grandparents' brothers and sisters. I'm very glad I did.

Soon after I started my research, I had some luck. I came across an old box of letters and photographs in the attic of my parents' home. Wedding photos, holiday photos, people I knew and people I didn't know. My grandmother had a sister who grew up in England and went to Canada when she was 18. When I saw her photos, I was sure that it was my grandmother. **3**__ I asked my mum if they were twins, but they weren't. They certainly looked similar to each other. There were some photos of my grandmother's sister's husband. He was an amazing man. He did wing walking on old planes. It was a dangerous way to earn a living and the people who did it were very popular. In one of the photos there's a big crowd of people around him asking for autographs. He looks like a rock star!

When my one-year subscription ran out, I gave up. I didn't go back as far as I wanted, and, apart from my great-uncle, I didn't discover any famous or talented relatives. **4**__ I definitely recommend it to anyone who is interested in history.

Below are some links to websites you may find useful. Good luck!

5G WRITING | An informal email

Open the email.	**Hi Gina,**
Say who it is about.	[1]*Who / How* are you? [2]*Think / Guess* what! I'm now studying Italian after school. I went to my first lesson [3]*last / ago* week. I really enjoyed it. The teacher is from Rome and her name is Violetta.
Describe the person's appearance.	She's very pretty and slim with long, wavy black hair and dark eyes. She looks a bit [4]*like / similar* the actress Demi Lovato. She seemed quite nervous at [5]*first / start* but when she started teaching, she was very calm and patient.
Describe the person's character.	
Talk about the person's interests.	She's only 22 and came to England to study literature at university. She loves Shakespeare and [6]*often goes / goes often* to the theatre to see his plays.
Talk about things you have in common.	She also loves cooking, like me, and she told me how to make a perfect pizza at home. Do you [7]*fancy / want* coming round at the weekend to cook Violetta's pizza? Text me!
Suggest something to do together.	Bye for now,
End the email.	Jemima

1
Read the email and complete the profile below.

Name: [1]*Violetta*

Home town: [2]_____

Hair: [3]_____

Eyes: [4]_____

Age: [5]_____

Subject studying: [6]_____

2
Read the email again and choose the correct words to complete it.

3
Match questions 1–3 with pieces of information a–f. There are two pieces of information for each question.

1 ☐☐ What does she look like?

2 ☐☐ What does she like?

3 ☐☐ What is she like?

a cooking   d Shakespeare

b calm   e patient

c pretty   f slim

4
Read the answers and complete the questions using the word *like*.

1 *What do you like doing* in your free time?

Playing football, listening to music and watching films.

2 _____?

My mum? She's funny and happy. She's very friendly.

3 _____?

My dad's quite tall and well-built. He's got short, grey hair and blue eyes.

4 _____?

My dog is small, brown with very short legs.

5 _____?

I like French, English and History.

5
WRITING TASK Write an email to your friend about a new neighbour. Use your imagination if you don't have a new neighbour in real life.

ACTIVE WRITING | An informal email

1 Plan your email.
- Think of when the person moved in and when you first met them.
- Think about the person's appearance, character and interests.
- Compare their appearance to a famous person.
- Think of a suggestion to make to the friend you are writing to.

2 Write the email.
- Open the email in a friendly way.
- Use the next three paragraphs to organise your email.
- Use the Past Simple to say when and where you first met the person.
- Use the Present Simple to give facts about the person's appearance, personality and likes.

3 Check that ...
- you have included all the relevant information.
- there are no spelling or grammar mistakes.
- you have used relevant topic vocabulary.

UNIT VOCABULARY PRACTICE

1 **5A GRAMMAR AND VOCABULARY** Match the adjectives from the box with the descriptions of people below.

confident   creative   funny   ~~helpful~~   patient   serious

1 Mark goes shopping with his mum twice a week. He also helps his younger sister with the homework at weekends. *helpful*

2 Our teacher never gets angry when students are late. When we cannot understand something, she always explains everything again. _____

3 Julie always makes her friends laugh. She would like to be a comedian one day. _____

4 Peter paints amazing pictures. Last month he won a prize for young artists. _____

5 Martha is always the first to put her hand up when the teacher asks a question. She likes giving a presentation in front of the whole class. _____

6 Tom is a quiet boy. In his free time, he likes studying astronomy. He never does silly things or tells jokes in class. _____

2 **5B VOCABULARY** Can you wear these clothes at the same time? Tick those that can go together and cross those that can't.

1 ☒ boots and shoes
2 ☐ shoes and socks
3 ☐ trousers and a coat
4 ☐ a dress and a skirt
5 ☐ a jacket and a shirt
6 ☐ trainers and boots
7 ☐ jeans and trousers
8 ☐ tracksuit bottoms and trainers
9 ☐ gloves and a scarf

3 **5B VOCABULARY** Complete the sentences with the words from the box.

attractive   bald   beard   eyes   fair   ~~short~~   slim   wavy

1 Selina isn't tall, she's quite *short*.
2 Is Suzanne pretty? Yes, she's very _____.
3 Jake eats a lot but he's still very _____.
4 My hair isn't dark. It's _____.
5 I've got very short hair but I'm not _____.
6 My dad's got a nice smile but you can't see it because of his big _____.
7 I've got straight hair, but I'd like it to be _____.
8 Emily has got lovely, big, brown _____.

4 **5E LISTENING AND VOCABULARY** Complete the dialogues with the correct forms of *fit*, *suit*, *go* or *match*.

Jemima I love this dress! It really **1***suits* me but I haven't got any shoes to **2**_____ with it.

Teresa Really? Your white shoes **3**_____ it well.

Jemima They're really old. I bought them when I was a size 36. They don't **4**_____ me now.

Michelle Do you think this skirt **5**_____ me?

Sabrina Yes, and it **6**_____ with that top. Does it **7**_____ you well?

Michelle Well, it's a bit small.

Alec You should buy this jumper. The colour **8**_____ your skirt.

Tom Yes, I like it, but I don't think they've got one that **9**_____ me. These are all too big.

5 **5F READING AND VOCABULARY** Complete the second sentence so that it means the same as the first one.

1 The twin brothers looked exactly the same.
The twin brothers were i*dentical*.

2 My family are all tall and have blond hair. I'm short with dark hair.
I l_____ d_____ from the rest of my family.

3 My sister and I both have long blond hair and blue eyes. We are tall and slim.
I l_____ l_____my sister.

4 I'm very easy-going and so is my brother.
I'm very easy-going. My brother is the s_____ as me.

5 Some people say that my brother's hair and eyes are like my dad's.
Some people say that my brother looks s_____ to my dad.

6 Marta is my best friend, but she is confident and I'm very shy.
Marta is my best friend, but she is very d_____ f_____ me.

7 People sometimes think Mark is the famous footballer Leo Messi.
Mark is Leo Messi's l_____.

6 **ON A HIGH NOTE** Write about your favourite clothes. When did you get them, when do you usually wear them and why do you like them?

1 For each learning objective, write 1–5 to assess your ability.

1 = I don't feel confident. 5 = I feel confident.

	Learning objective	Course material	How confident I am (1–5)
5A	I can use the Past Simple to talk about the past.	Student's Book pp. 64–65 Workbook pp. 52–53	
5B	I can talk about people's appearance and clothes.	Student's Book p. 66 Workbook p. 54	
5C	I can shop for clothes.	Student's Book p. 67 Workbook p. 55	
5D	I can use the Past Simple to ask questions and give affirmative or negative answers.	Student's Book p. 68 Workbook p. 56	
5E	I can identify specific information in an interview and talk about clothes.	Student's Book p. 69 Workbook p. 57	
5F	I can understand the structure of a text and talk about family and lookalikes.	Student's Book pp. 70–71 Workbook pp. 58–59	
5G	I can write an informal email.	Student's Book p. 72 Workbook p. 60	

2 Which of the skills above would you like to improve in? How?

Skill I want to improve in	How I can improve

3 What can you remember from this unit?

New words I learned and most want to remember	Expressions and phrases I liked	English I heard or read outside class

GRAMMAR AND VOCABULARY

1 Complete the text with the correct words formed from the words in bold.

> Hi Sonia,
>
> How are you? I promised in my last email to tell you about my friend Adrianna.
>
> She's an amazing person. She's got a great ¹*personality* (PERSON). She's very ²_____ (CREATE) and has a great imagination. She's always thinking of wonderful ideas. She's also very kind and ³_____ (HELP).
>
> I also love her appearance. She's very ⁴_____ (ATTRACT). She has big blue eyes, a nice smile and blond, ⁵_____ (CURL) hair. It isn't surprising, her mum is really ⁶_____ (BEAUTY) too.
>
> Next time, I'll tell you about my school. Write soon,
>
> Amy

/ 5

2 Complete the sentences with one word in each gap.

1 My dad is very good-looking. He <u>looks</u> like a film star!
2 Our new teacher is about 40 or 50 years old. I'm not sure exactly, but he's m_____ -a_____.
3 Your shirt g_____ well with that jacket.
4 Can I borrow your g_____? My hands are really cold.
5 I wear shoes to school, boots for long walks and t_____ for playing sports.
6 It's strange. All my family have got dark hair, but I've got f_____ hair.

/ 5

3 Complete the sentences with the correct Past Simple forms of the words in brackets.

1 Who <u>was</u> (be) your best friend when you <u>were</u> (be) at primary school?
2 _____ (you/enjoy) the book I _____ (give) you?
3 We _____ (not laugh) because the joke _____ (not be) funny.
4 Salim _____ (go) to the shops but they _____ (not be) open.
5 My brother and I _____ (be) identical a few years ago but his hair _____ (change) colour last year.
6 _____ (your girlfriend/wear) her new hat yesterday? You know, the one you _____ (buy) her for her birthday?

/ 5

4 Use the prompts to write sentences in the Past Simple.

1 Where / you buy / those shoes?
Where did you buy those shoes?
2 How many languages / can / your grandfather / speak / when he / be / a boy?
_____
3 I / not like / the film / we see / last night
_____
4 When / you start / learning the piano?
_____
5 Who / be / that woman in the classroom?
_____
6 When I / be / young / I always / want / to be a firefighter
_____

/ 5

USE OF ENGLISH

5 Complete the second sentence so that it means the same as the first one. Use no more than three words.

1 My uncle has got blue eyes.
My *uncle's eyes are* blue.
2 My friend and I both like a lot of the same things.
My friend and I have got a _____ common.
3 I love this dress. I'd like to see what I look like in it.
I love this dress. I'd like to _____ on.
4 Amir's dad has got no hair at all but he's very good-looking.
Amir's dad is _____ but he's very good-looking.
5 Marie and her mother don't look the same at all.
Marie looks completely _____ her mother.
6 Can you describe Ben's appearance?
What _____ like?

/ 5

6 Choose the correct words a–c to complete the text.

A book that inspired me was *Louder than Words* by Laura Jarratt. I'm not very good ¹__ talking to people so it ²__ great to find a book about a girl, Rafaela, who can't speak at all. Her brother was ³__ my brother. He helped her and slowly she became more ⁴__ and started speaking. In the end, her brother needed help and Rafaela was there for him. My brother helps me too, but I hope he doesn't have the ⁵__ kind of problems that Rafaela's brother had!

1 a at   **b** in   **c** for
2 a were   **b** did   **c** was
3 a similar   **b** same   **c** like
4 a kind   **b** confident   **c** creative
5 a identical   **b** same   **c** similar

/ 5

/ 30

06 The arts around us

6A GRAMMAR AND VOCABULARY

Comparative and superlative adjectives

1 ⭐ Choose the correct words to complete the sentences.

1 I think the cinema is *more / most* exciting than the theatre.
2 Van Gogh's 'Starry Night' is the *better / best* painting in this museum.
3 Madonna, who's a famous singer, is as *old / older* as my grandmother!
4 *Iron Man* is *cooler / coolest* than *Spiderman*.
5 Pop music isn't as relaxing *as / than* classical music.

2 ⭐ Complete the sentences with the correct forms of the adjectives in brackets.

1 Beethoven's music is <u>more dramatic</u> (dramatic) than Mozart's.
2 Books about wizards aren't as _____ (interesting) as books about real people.
3 The film was _____ (bad) than I expected.
4 I think *Skyfall* was the _____ (popular) James Bond film.
5 Shakespeare's plays are _____ (easy) to read than Dicken's novels.

3 ⭐⭐ Read the texts and complete the information.

4 ⭐⭐ Put the words in order to make sentences.

1 in / cheapest / shop / the / was / painting / the / this
This was the cheapest painting in the shop.
2 one / bigger / old / than / is / our new / our / TV
_____
3 better / the / singing / was / than / the dancing
_____
4 the / in / the / sculpture / museum / this / is / strangest
_____
5 as / wasn't / actress / talented / the / the actor / as
_____
6 colour / are / photos / than / black and white / more / photos / interesting
_____
7 greatest / world / the / director / the / Steven Spielberg / in / is / ?
_____

My favourite books are *Frankenstein*, *Dracula* and *Treasure Island*. *Treasure Island* is older than *Dracula* but it isn't as old as *Frankenstein*. *Frankenstein* is the oldest of the three books.

Books – written in:

1818: ¹<u>Frankenstein</u>
1883: ² _____
1897: ³ _____

I like reading film reviews. They are very useful. My favourite website says that the 2017 *Spiderman* is better than *Iron Man*. It also says that *Logan* isn't as good as *Iron Man*.

Website film reviews:

***** Brilliant: ⁴ _____
**** Very good: ⁵ _____
** OK: ⁶ _____

The price of paintings is crazy. The most expensive paintig was 'Salvator Mundi' by Leonardo da Vinci. 'The Card Players' by Cézanne was also very expensive but not as expensive as 'Interchange' by Willem de Kooning.

Price of paintings:

$450 million: ⁷ _____
$300 million: ⁸ _____
$250 million: ⁹ _____

5 ★★ Complete the questions with the words from the box. Then read the answers below.

as   more   ~~oldest~~   than   the   worst

1 Where is the _oldest_ painting in the world?
2 What's _____ longest running play in the world?
3 Was Elvis Presley _____ successful than the Beatles?
4 Is Brad Pitt _____ tall as George Clooney?
5 Is Van Gogh's 'Sunflowers' painting older _____ his 'Starry Night' painting?
6 What is the _____ film ever made?

Exercise 5 key
(1) In a cave in Indonesia. It's 35,000 years old. 2 *The Mousetrap.* It started in London in 1952 and it's still on now. 3 No, he wasn't. The Beatles sold 42 million more albums than Elvis. 4 Yes. They are both 1.80 m tall. 5 Yes. His most famous 'Sunflowers' painting is from 1888 and 'Starry Night' is from 1889. 6 Everyone has different opinions, but *Saving Christmas* has the lowest score on IMDB website.)

6 ★★ USE OF ENGLISH Complete the text with one word in each gap.

100 TOP BOOKS FOR TEENAGERS

We asked teenagers about their favourite books. Not surprisingly, the ¹*most* popular books were the *Harry Potter* stories. *The Hunger Games* books weren't ²_____ popular as *Harry Potter* but they were ³_____ popular than the other books. In third place was *To Kill a Mockingbird*. This came out in 1960 but it wasn't ⁴_____ oldest book on the list. That was *The Hobbit* which came out in 1937. *The Hobbit* was 5th in the list and was more popular ⁵_____ *The Lord of the Rings* which finished in 7th place. I wonder which film version of these books is the ⁶_____ popular?

Read the full list of 100 top books for teenagers below.

7 ★★ USE OF ENGLISH Complete the second sentence using the word in bold so that it means the same as the first one. Use no more than three words including the word in bold.

1 Last year's concert was better than this year's. **AS**
This year's concert wasn't _as good as_ last year's.
2 This photo isn't as bright as that one. **DARKER**
This photo _____ that one.
3 No day last year was hotter than June 20th. **THE**
June 20th _____ day last year.
4 My bedroom isn't as tidy as yours. **THAN**
Your bedroom _____ mine.
5 The play wasn't as good as I hoped. **THAN**
The play was _____ I hoped.
6 None of the students is as talented as Rita. **MOST**
Rita is _____ student.

8 ★★★ USE OF ENGLISH Choose the correct forms to complete the text.

Kröller Müller

Why is the Kröller-Müller museum in the Netherlands my favourite art gallery? First of all, it's in the middle of a park. ¹__ thing about going there is that there are bikes in the park, and you can take one and cycle through the forest. The gallery has a lot of Van Gogh's paintings. I think they are ²__ interesting than his paintings in Paris and Amsterdam because they ³__ famous as those paintings. It's nice to see something new. ⁴__ popular Van Gogh's painting in the museum is his 'Terrace of a Café at Night'. I think it's the most beautiful painting in the world! I love it.

There's also a sculpture garden. I don't think the sculptures are as fascinating ⁵__ the paintings but on a summer day it's ⁶__ to be outside than inside. The museum is more expensive than other museums and galleries but I love going there.

1 a As good as	b Better	c The best
2 a as	b more	c most
3 a are as	b aren't as	c are more
4 a As	b The more	c The most
5 a as	b than	c that
6 a as nice	b nicer	c the nicest

9 ON A HIGH NOTE Compare two of your favourite books or songs. Write at least five sentences using different adjectives and comparisons.

1 Read the blog quickly. Complete the table with the information about the three street art festivals.

	Town	Country	Month(s)
1	*Asilah*		
2			
3			

2 Read the blog again and choose the correct answers.

1 Which sentence is true about Asilah?
   a It's a good place to visit for eating.
   b The local festival lasts two months.
   c The festival is for painters only.

2 Most visitors to Genalguacil's art festival
   a stay the night.
   b drive there by car.
   c also enjoy the weather.

3 What does the author say about Tartu?
   a There is a film show as part of every Stencibility.
   b June is a good time to go to the festival.
   c The city is unattractive.

4 Which of these is an advert for the three art festivals?
   a Come to these world-famous art festivals which take place in July and August.
   b See some great street art and try local food in these little-known locations across Europe.
   c Enjoy great art and discover some amazing little towns.

Vocabulary extension

3 Match the highlighted verbs from the text with the definitions.

1 Arrive at a place. *turn up*
2 Organise a concert, play or a film show. _____
3 Go on foot with no special place to get to. _____
4 Happen after being planned. _____
5 Become something different. _____

4 Complete the sentences with the correct forms of the verbs from Exercise 3.

1 Only ten people *turned up* for a dance at school.
2 On the first day of our holiday we just _____ the town centre to see what it was like.
3 The film festival _____ in October.
4 The students _____ a play at school last month.
5 John is quite shy but when he stands in front of an audience, he _____ a star!

ACTIVE VOCABULARY
Forming adjectives from verbs and nouns

We can form adjectives from verbs and nouns by adding a suffix. Here are three suffixes we often use to form adjectives:

• Verb + -ing (e.g. *to interest – interesting*)
• Noun + -y (e.g. *wind – windy, mess – messy*)
• Noun + -ly (e.g. *love – lovely*)

Sometimes the spelling is different (e.g. *to surprise – surprising*).

5 Complete the sentences with the correct adjectives formed from the words in bold. Be careful with the spelling of some of the adjectives.

1 I love this village. It's a *lovely* place to stay in the summer. **LOVE**
2 It's really _____ here. There's nothing to do. **BORE**
3 We had an _____ time in Croatia. We loved it there! **AMAZE**
4 Let's eat here. The food is great and the owners are very _____. **FRIEND**
5 I love this book about Picasso. It's very _____. **INTEREST**
6 I'm going to go home. I feel really _____. **SLEEP**
7 We were very _____ because we got free tickets for the exhibition. **LUCK**
8 We learned some _____ facts about the paintings in the gallery. **SURPRISE**

6 ON A HIGH NOTE Write about a festival in your town or in your country.

UNIT VOCABULARY PRACTICE > page 73

STREET ART

Today I'd like to tell you about street art and some of the amazing places where you can see works of art as you walk around the town.

• • •

Let's start in Asilah, a small and sleepy town on Morocco's north-west coast. There's little to do there when the sun goes down but for one month a year, in July or August, the town turns into an art gallery. Artists turn up to paint awesome pictures on the white walls of the houses and the town becomes very colourful.

Other artists come to Asilah too. You can watch talented dancers and listen to poetry in the streets. And, of course, you can eat tasty Moroccan food in the restaurants in the old town. Asilah is a lovely place and many people go back at other times of year to enjoy the peace and quiet.

Another town which is like a living art gallery is Genalguacil in the south of Spain. This is a tiny place which some people may find a little boring. However, for art lovers, for two weeks in August, it's the perfect place to go. As you walk through the streets you can see sculptures everywhere. There are also street performances to entertain visitors. Buses bring tourists up the road from the coast to look at art and to enjoy the cooler temperatures and clean air up in the hills. Most visitors come on day trips but there are one or two places to stay. You can then enjoy the empty streets after all the tour buses depart.

Not all of the best festivals take place in the south. One of the most interesting street art festivals is called Stencibility. It takes place in Tartu in Estonia. Tartu isn't as big or beautiful as Tallinn, the capital of Estonia, although it's still very interesting and the people are friendly. The organisers try to offer different activities each year that visitors can enjoy in addition to the street art. One year they put on film shows, another year they organise talks and guided tours so that visitors can learn more about the city, the festival and the artists. You may even meet some of the artists as you look around the city. This festival takes place in June when the days in Estonia are very long and the weather is beautiful.

Do you know of any other street art festivals? Let me know. I'd love to know about them.

6C VOCABULARY | Films

1 ★ Match the adjectives from the box with the descriptions.

big-budget   disappointing   exciting   ~~funny~~
low-budget   original   predictable   scary

1 It makes people laugh. *funny*
2 It was a very expensive film to make. _____
3 The ending was obvious from the start. _____
4 There were lots of great action scenes – I couldn't stop watching it. _____
5 I closed my eyes because I was so frightened! _____
6 I was really excited before I went to see it, but it wasn't as good as I thought. _____
7 It was a completely different kind of story to the normal Hollywood film. _____
8 It didn't cost much money at all. _____

2 ★ Complete the sentences with types of films.

1 *A Star is Born*: My mum loved this d**rama**. It was about love, but it was very sad. My mum cried at the end.
2 Pixar and Disney make a lot of a_____ films like *Toy Story* and *Frozen*.
3 *Crazy Rich Asians* was a c_____. It was very funny. It was also a r_____ because the characters fall in love. We call this kind of film a 'romcom'.
4 Peter Jackson is a famous director. He made the f_____ films *Lord of the Rings* and *The Hobbit*. He also made a d_____ about the First World War using real film taken over 100 years ago.
5 Marvel films are s_____ films, but you could also call them a_____ films because there are good guys fighting bad guys.
6 Most h_____ films are for people aged 18 or over but *The Ring* was for 15-year-olds and older, so I saw it. It was very scary.
7 I liked *The Greatest Showman*. It was a good m_____. My parents bought a CD of the songs from the film and they play it all the time.
8 My friends love *Star Wars* but I'm not keen on s_____ f_____ films.
9 I saw *The Ballad of Buster Scruggs* yesterday. Buster Scruggs is a cowboy with a horse called Dan, so this is a w_____, but it's also quite funny and has songs.

3 ★★ Complete the questions with some of the words from Exercise 2.

What's worse?

1 A boring *documentary* about the life of someone you don't know or an _____ film which is really for five-year-olds?
2 A _____ film that isn't frightening or a _____ with an actor and actress who obviously don't love each other?
3 A _____ film set in space with bad special effects or a _____ film about wizards and dragons with a terrible plot?
4 A predictable _____ film which is part of a long series (*Spiderman 8, Iron Man 6*) or an _____ film about police officers and gangsters with actors who are really singers and aren't very good at acting.
5 A _____ that isn't funny or a _____ with terrible songs?

4 ★★ Complete the dialogue with the words from the box.

audience   cast   character   ending   ~~plot~~   scene
soundtrack   special effects

Simon This comedy film festival is a great idea. It's nice to see films which are a few years old. How was the film last night? I missed it.
Brad It was OK. It had a good [1]*plot*. It was about Hollywood in the 1950's and an actor who goes missing. It was quite funny.
Simon Who was in the [2]_____?
Brad Lots of famous people. George Clooney, Scarlet Johansson and more. George Clooney's [3]_____ was funny. He was a famous but not a very good actor! The best [4]_____ was when he couldn't remember his lines.
Simon Were there any spectacular [5]_____?
Brad I'm sure they used some, but it wasn't a science fiction film with spaceships or aliens.
Simon What about the [6]_____?
Brad It wasn't very special. There was one nice tune that Channing Tatum danced to, but I don't want to buy the CD! I liked the [7]_____. It was a good way to finish the film. And I think the other people in the [8]_____ liked it. People laughed and they all looked happy as we walked out of the cinema.

5 ON A HIGH NOTE Use some of the words from this lesson to write about the kind of films you like and dislike and explain why.

6D GRAMMAR

Too, (not) enough

1 ★ Complete the answers with *Yes* or *No*.

1 Is this TV OK for you?

a *No*, it's too big.

b _____, it's big enough.

c _____, it isn't big enough.

2 Is the actor's voice right for the film?

a _____, it's loud enough.

b _____, it isn't loud enough.

c _____, it's too loud.

3 Was the film a good length?

a _____, it was too long.

b _____, it wasn't long enough.

c _____, it was long enough.

2 ★ Complete the sentences with *too* or *enough*.

Message from: B. Bruckerhorn, Producer

Topic: New big-budget film

I saw the new film yesterday. It's awful!
The plot is ¹*too* predictable.
The film is ² _____ long.
The action isn't exciting ³ _____.
The characters aren't interesting ⁴ _____.
The music is ⁵ _____ loud.
The director wasn't brave ⁶ _____.
The main actor is ⁷ _____ short.
The main actress isn't talented ⁸ _____.

Luckily, I'm rich ⁹ _____ to pay for some changes
and I'm experienced ¹⁰ _____ to know what to do.
We need a new director, a new cast, new writers,
new soundtrack composers and better special effects.
I can give you $200 million and three months. I want
this film to be the most successful in history!

---

3 ★★ Complete the sentences with the correct adjectives from the pairs of words in the box.

---

big / small   busy / free   difficult / easy   early / late
funny / serious   ~~noisy / quiet~~   old / young

---

1 I can't work when other people talk and play music at the same time. It's too *noisy* to concentrate.

2 I haven't got time to help you today. I'm too _____.

3 You can't go into the cinema. You're too _____. The film started five minutes ago.

4 I can't understand this book. It's too _____ for me.

5 I'm not _____ enough to see this film. It's for over 18's only.

6 You can't see all the paintings in the museum in one day. It's too _____.

7 It wasn't a good comedy. It wasn't _____ enough.

4 ★★★ USE OF ENGLISH Complete the second sentence using the word in bold so that it means the same as the first one. Use no more than three words including the word in bold.

1 I'm too poor to make a film. **RICH**

I'm *not rich enough* to make a film.

2 I couldn't finish the test. I wasn't fast enough. **SLOW**

I couldn't finish the test. I _____.

3 The laptop I wanted wasn't cheap enough. **EXPENSIVE**

The laptop I wanted _____.

4 The actors are too quiet and I can't hear them. **LOUD**

The actors aren't _____ and I can't hear them.

5 This tablet isn't small enough for my bag. **BIG**

This tablet _____ for my bag.

6 The old cinema is too cold and people don't like going there. **WARM**

The old cinema isn't _____ and people don't like going there.

5 ON A HIGH NOTE Write about films, books, songs, bands or types of art that you don't like and say why using *too* or *enough*.

6E LISTENING AND VOCABULARY

1 Choose the correct words to complete the sentences.

1 When people want to buy or sell something like a famous painting, they usually do it at __.

a an auction   **b** a museum   **c** a festival

2 When you have a painting or a photograph and you want to put it on a wall, you usually put a thin piece of wood or plastic around it. We call this a __.

a cover   **b** sculpture   **c** frame

2 ◁ᴗ *41* **Listen to an interview and choose the correct answers.**

1 What does the presenter say about Banksy?

a You can only see his paintings in Britain.

b He is now well-known in many countries.

c People recognise him wherever he goes.

2 What do we know about 'Balloon Girl'?

a Justin Bieber bought a copy of the painting.

b All versions of the picture are identical.

c Banksy signed some of the copies of the painting.

3 We definitely know that

a 'Balloon Girl' wasn't the only painting on sale that day.

b the person who bought it was at the auction.

c Banksy was at the auction.

4 What do we know about the joke?

a No-one knows who planned it.

b It destroyed the whole painting.

c It didn't go exactly as planned.

5 What was the buyer's reaction?

a She was happy in the end.

b She sold the painting for £2 million.

c She tried to get her money back.

Vocabulary extension

3 ◁ᴗ *42* **Complete the extracts from the recording in Exercise 2 with adverbs formed from the adjectives in the box. Listen and check.**

complete   ~~easy~~   lucky   slow   sudden

1 No-one knows who he is, but you can *easily* recognise his paintings.

2 _____, there was a noise.

3 The painting started to move _____ downwards.

4 It was a big joke by Banksy but _____ something went wrong.

5 The machine stopped before it destroyed the painting _____.

4 ON A HIGH NOTE **What could you sell at an auction? Describe it and make it sound as attractive as possible.**

Pronunciation

ACTIVE PRONUNCIATION | /dʒ/ and /g/ sounds

You can hear the sound /dʒ/ in words with the letters *j*, *g* and *dg* (e.g. *jam*, *generous*, *budget*).

Be careful, the letter *g* can be /dʒ/ or /g/, (e.g. a*g*e, hun*g*ry).

5 ◁ᴗ *43* **Listen to the underlined words and repeat them. Which word doesn't have the /dʒ/ sound?**

Waterloo <u>Bridge</u>

<u>Justin</u> Bieber

Balloon <u>Girl</u>

something <u>strange</u>

a big <u>joke</u>

6 ◁ᴗ *44* **Look at more words. Tick the ones which we pronounce with the /dʒ/ sound. Listen, check and repeat.**

1 ☐ August   **5** ☐ village

2 ☑ gym   **6** ☐ middle-aged

3 ☐ Biology   **7** ☐ yoghurt

4 ☐ magazine   **8** ☐ gender

7 ◁ᴗ *45* **Listen to some words which contain two letters *g*. Find the letter *g* which has the /dʒ/ sound.**

1 garage

2 language

3 Geography

4 changing

8 ◁ᴗ *46* **Listen to ten words that contain the /dʒ/ sound and write them in the correct column.**

/dʒ/ sound spelled with *j*	/dʒ/ sound spelled with *g*	/dʒ/ sound spelled with *dg*
juice		

UNIT VOCABULARY PRACTICE > page 73

6F SPEAKING

1 🔊 **47** Listen and repeat the phrases. How do you say them in your language?

SPEAKING | Suggestions

MAKING SUGGESTIONS

What/How about playing tennis?

Why don't we go shopping?

Let's go out.

ACCEPTING SUGGESTIONS

That's a good idea.

Yes, why not?

OK, let's do that.

Sounds good/great/amazing.

REFUSING SUGGESTIONS

No way! (informal)

I don't think that's a great idea.

I don't think so.

I'm not sure.

SUGGESTING AN ALTERNATIVE

Why don't we watch a film **instead**?

Let's play a computer game **instead**.

---

2 Choose the correct words to complete the mini-conversations.

Sandy   What shall we do today?

Kerry   How about **¹**go / going to the cinema?

Sandy   Yes, why **²**no / not?

John   What do you want to do today?

Vicky   Why don't we **³**go / going to a museum?

John   No **⁴**way / think so. Let's stay at home instead.

Lucy   Do you want to meet up today?

Kate   OK. Let's **⁵**play / playing my new computer game.

Lucy   I don't think that's a great **⁶**thought / idea. Why **⁷**not / don't we go shopping instead?

Kate   OK. **⁸**Sound / Sounds great.

3 Match the sentence beginnings with the endings.

A

1 ☐ How about   **a** go out later.

2 ☐ Let's   **b** we go out later?

3 ☐ Why don't   **c** going out later?

B

1 ☐ That's a good   **a** not?

2 ☐ Yes, why   **b** idea.

3 ☐ OK. Let's do   **c** that.

C

1 ☐ I don't think   **a** sure.

2 ☐ I'm not   **b** instead.

3 ☐ Let's go out   **c** so.

4 Put the sentences in order to make a conversation.

a ☐ **Boris**   No way! It's Saturday. Let's go shopping instead.

b ☐ **Boris**   I'm not sure. It's a long way. Why don't we get the bus instead?

c ☐ **Boris**   I'm bored.

d ☐ **Teresa**   OK. Let's do that. Shall we walk?

e ☐ **Teresa**   That's a good idea. Come on then.

f ☐ **Teresa**   How about doing some homework?

5 🔊 **48** Complete the mini-conversations with one word or contraction in each gap. Listen and check.

Nathan   Why **¹**_don't_ we take some photos of the animals in the park?

Jasmine   OK, **²**_____ do that.

Phil   What shall we do today?

Roma   What **³**_____ checking out the new art shop?

Phil   Yes, **⁴**_____ not?

Uli   Do you want to go for a coffee?

Sonia   I'm not **⁵**_____. I haven't got much money. Why don't we have coffee at my house **⁶**_____?

Uli   That's a good **⁷**_____.

Jasmine   Shall we phone Jack?

Lena   I don't think **⁸**_____. He's very busy at the moment. Let's phone Lizzie instead. Her band are playing on Saturday. We can ask her for tickets.

Jasmine   OK. **⁹**_____ good. Let's **¹⁰**_____ that.

MY FAVOURITE SCOTTISH FILM

| Give general information about the film. |

Local Hero is a comedy drama film by the Scottish director Bill Forsyth. The cast includes the American actor Burt Lancaster and a lot of great Scottish actors including Peter Capaldi. The film came out in 1983 but it still looks great today. Bill Forsyth ¹_____ a BAFTA award for best direction and a New York film award for best screenplay. In 2019, there was a new musical play based on the film.

| Describe characters and story. |

The film is ²_____ in the village of Ferness in Scotland. It's a quiet place near the sea and the mountains and life is very slow there. The ³_____ is very simple. An American oil executive comes to Scotland to buy the village for his oil business. At first he finds the people there strange but he is slowly falling in love with the village and isn't sure that he wants to change it.

| Give your opinion. |

The film isn't the sort of film that makes you laugh a lot but it makes you feel happy. The ⁴_____ in the village are all interesting and the views of Scotland are beautiful. I think it is the best film there is about life in Scotland. ⁵_____ I would recommend this film to anyone who likes quiet, slow-paced films without special effects and lots of action.

| Summarise. |

1 Read the review and complete the notes.

Title:	¹*Local Hero*
Director:	²_____
Actors:	³_____ and ⁴_____
Set in:	⁵_____ in Scotland
Main characters:	An American ⁶_____ and people from the village in Scotland
Type of film:	⁷_____
Reviewer's opinions:	It makes you ⁸_____

2 USE OF ENGLISH Choose the correct words a–c to complete the review.

1 a won   **b** took   **c** found
2 a set   **b** taken   **c** made
3 a scene   **b** cast   **c** plot
4 a cast   **b** characters   **c** actors
5 a Overall   **b** Always   **c** Last

3 Complete the plot of *Local Hero* with the correct present forms of the verbs in brackets.

Local Hero is a film about different cultures. Mac ¹*is* (be) a businessman from Texas who ²_____ (try) to buy a village in Scotland. He ³_____ (spend) several weeks in the village and ⁴_____ (slowly/fall) in love with the place and its interesting residents.

Most people in the village want to sell their homes and become rich but one man ⁵_____ (not want) to leave his small home on the beach. How does it end? ⁶_____ the oil company _____ (destroy) the village to look for oil? Why not watch it and see?

4 WRITING TASK Write a review of your favourite film from your country or one that you think is important for people to see.

ACTIVE WRITING | A film review

1 Plan your review.
- Choose the film you want to write about.
- Make notes about the director, actors and any awards the film won.
- Think about the plot and main characters.
- Make notes about your opinions and adjectives to describe the film.
- Say why you think it is important and who you think would enjoy it.

2 Write the review.
- Start by saying the title of the film and the director's name.
- Organise the review into three paragraphs: general information, the plot, your opinions.
- Use present tenses to describe the plot.

3 Check that …
- you have included all the relevant information.
- there are no spelling or grammar mistakes.

UNIT VOCABULARY PRACTICE

1 6A GRAMMAR AND VOCABULARY Match the words from the box with the comments.

dance film literature ~~music~~ painting photography sculpture theatre

1 I love this song. The music is brilliant, and the singer has got a great voice. _music_

2 The actor was very unhappy when a phone started ringing. He stopped speaking and looked angrily at the audience. _____

3 It's a great book. The writing is amazing. _____

4 The director's great, the special effects are awesome, and the soundtrack is brilliant. _____

5 What is this? It's a strange stone shape. It looks like a person, but it hasn't got a head. _____

6 We need a choreographer to help us get the moves right. _____

7 I'm not keen on modern art. I prefer looking at the work of da Vinci and Rembrandt. _____

8 I love these. They show people at work or in the street and they are all in black and white. _____

2 6B READING AND VOCABULARY Choose the correct words to complete the sentences. Sometimes more than one answer is correct.

1 These cakes are __. Can I have another one?
  a awful **b** delicious **c** disgusting

2 How much money do you __ for working in the restaurant?
  a earn **b** take **c** pay

3 It was __ party! Thanks for inviting me!
  a an awesome **b** a brilliant **c** a talented

4 The show was __. I fell asleep.
  a awesome **b** boring **c** awful

5 The sandwiches sold __ before we arrived at the café.
  a up **b** out **c** away

6 It's __ film. Go and see it!
  a a brilliant **b** a luxurious **c** an awful

3 6C VOCABULARY Complete the text with the words from the box.

audience ~~budget~~ cast effects ending funny plot
predictable scary soundtrack

The latest big- **1**_budget_ film from top film director Jane Cameron was OK. The **2**_____ in the cinema loved it. They laughed at the **3**_____ parts, they screamed at the **4**_____ parts. The special **5**_____ were amazing and all the actors and actresses in the **6**_____ were excellent. So, why wasn't it as good as I hoped?

Well, the **7**_____ was nothing new – in fact it was very **8**_____. I knew exactly who the killer was as soon as I saw him. I didn't like the **9**_____, either. The man got off the train and … that was it. The film finished.

The best thing for me was the **10**_____ which used some great old rock songs. My advice is to buy the CD and wait until the film is on TV.

4 6C VOCABULARY Label the pictures with the film genres from the box.

action fantasy horror musical romance
~~science fiction~~ superhero western

1 _science fiction_   **2** _____

3 _____   **4** _____

5 _____   **6** _____

7 _____   **8** _____

5 6E LISTENING AND VOCABULARY Replace *get* in the dialogues with the correct forms of *become*, *arrive*, *receive* or *buy*.

Ralf What time did you **1**_arrive_ (get) home?

Danny It was late. I stopped to **2**_____ (get) something to eat. When I **3**_____ (got) home, I woke my parents up and they **4**_____ (got) angry.

Mum Did you have a good day at school?

Beth No. My bus was late so I **5**_____ at (got to) school late. Then I **6**_____ (got) my mark for the Chemistry test. It wasn't good. I **7**_____ (got) a bit upset so on the way home I **8**_____ (got) a cake but I dropped it before I could eat it.

Mum You're lucky you didn't **9**_____ (get) a fine for dropping litter!

6 ON A HIGH NOTE Write about a day in your life and use three different meanings of *get* (e.g. *buy*, *receive* and *become*) in your text.

1 For each learning objective, write 1–5 to assess your ability.

1 = I don't feel confident. 5 = I feel confident.

	Learning objective	Course material	How confident I am (1–5)
6A	I can use comparative and superlative adjectives to talk about people or objects.	Student's Book pp. 76–77 Workbook pp. 64–65	
6B	I can understand new words in a text and talk about music festivals.	Student's Book pp. 78–79 Workbook pp. 66–67	
6C	I can talk about films.	Student's Book p. 80 Workbook p. 68	
6D	I can use *too* and (*not*) *enough* to talk about the quantity of something.	Student's Book p. 81 Workbook p. 69	
6E	I can identify specific information in an interview and talk about graffiti.	Student's Book p. 82 Workbook p. 70	
6F	I can make and accept or refuse suggestions.	Student's Book p. 83 Workbook p. 71	
6G	I can write a film review.	Student's Book p. 84 Workbook p. 72	

2 Which of the skills above would you like to improve in? How?

Skill I want to improve in	How I can improve

3 What can you remember from this unit?

New words I learned and most want to remember	Expressions and phrases I liked	English I heard or read outside class

Self-check

GRAMMAR AND VOCABULARY

1 Complete the sentences with the correct words formed from the words in bold.

1 The _director_ won an Oscar for his second film. **DIRECT**
2 We need someone who is _____ and hard-working. **COMMUNICATE**
3 I watched an interesting _____ about global warming. **DOCUMENT**
4 This drama school is great for people who want to become _____. **ACT**
5 The company booked a hotel for us. It was very _____. **LUXURY**
6 The plot was good, but the ending was a bit _____. **PREDICT**

/ 5

2 Complete the sentences with the words from the box. There are three extra words.

audience ~~cast~~ character choreographer composer plot scene scriptwriter soundtrack

1 All the actors in a film or play are the _cast_.
2 The people who watch a film or play are the _____.
3 A person who organises a dance routine for a show is a _____.
4 All the music or songs used in a film is called the _____.
5 The story of a book or film is also called the _____.
6 The person who writes a piece of music is a _____.

/ 5

3 Complete the sentences with one word in each gap.

1 The play we saw last week was better _than_ the one we saw last year.
2 I like the film, but it isn't _____ good as the book.
3 I think Sandra Bullock was _____ best actress in the film.
4 Tickets for the theatre are _____ expensive than tickets for the cinema.
5 I didn't have _____ time to buy popcorn before the film started.
6 The sculptures at the museum were _____ far away to see them properly.

/ 5

4 Match the two parts of the sentences.

1 ☐ I think science-fiction films are better
2 ☐ The most exciting
3 ☐ _Batman_ isn't as interesting
4 ☐ A lot of films are too
5 ☐ The lead actor's singing wasn't good

a enough for a musical.
b than fantasy films.
c long.
d _Star Wars_ film is _The Empire Strikes Back_.
e as _Spiderman_.

/ 5

USE OF ENGLISH

5 Complete the second sentence using the word in bold so that it means the same as the first one. Use no more than three words including the word in bold.

1 The actor wasn't tall enough for his part. He looked strange. **TOO**
The actor _was too short_ for his part. He looked strange.
2 The action in the film takes place in Moscow. **SET**
The film _____ Moscow.
3 The film was too serious for me. **FUNNY**
The film was _____ for me.
4 The guitar is easier to play than the piano. **AS**
The piano isn't _____ play as the guitar.
5 There's no better entertainment than a good concert. **THE**
A good concert is _____ of entertainment there is.
6 The concert hall didn't have any tickets left when we got there. **OUT**
All the tickets _____ when we got to the concert hall.

/ 5

6 Complete the text with the correct words formed from the words in bold.

Our art teacher is the ¹_best_ (**GOOD**) teacher in our school. She always encourages us to be ²_____ (**CREATE**) in our lessons. Her lessons are very interesting and ³_____ (**ORIGIN**). She gives us problems and puts us in groups to find a solution. She says that this will make us more imaginative, which will help to make our ⁴_____ (**PAINT**) more original. She says that she did the same thing at university and it helped her when she became a ⁵_____ (**SCULPTURE**). Unfortunately for her (but fortunately for us), although she was very ⁶_____ (**TALENT**), she didn't earn much money from art, so she became a teacher.

/ 5

/ 30

75

07 *Going to town*

7A GRAMMAR AND VOCABULARY

Going to

1 ⭐ **Choose the correct words to complete the sentences.**

1 Ellen *is / are* going to have a party next week.
2 I'm *going / going to* watch films all night.
3 Steve and Mark *is / are* going to go camping.
4 Michelle is going *make / to make* a cake.
5 We *don't / aren't* going to do any school work today.
6 Some students are going to *give / giving* the teachers flowers.

2 ⭐ **Read the questions and write short answers.**

1 Is your dad going to take you to the sports centre?
   ✓ *Yes, he is.*
2 Is your sister going to study Maths at university?
   ✓ _____
3 Are you going to eat in the town centre?
   ✗ _____
4 Are your parents going to sell their car?
   ✓ _____
5 Are you and your brother going to cycle to the seaside?
   ✓ _____
6 Are Jessica and Paula going to be in the school play?
   ✗ _____

3 ⭐ **Complete the mini-conversations with one word in each gap.**

Meg What ¹*are* you going to wear to the party?
Omri I don't know yet. Felix ² _____ going to help me choose something nice.

Omri How long are you going ³ _____ stay at the party?
Meg Not long. My dad is ⁴ _____ to collect me at ten o'clock.

Omri Hi, Felix. ⁵ _____ you going to walk to the party?
Felix No, I'm ⁶ _____. My mum's going to take me.

Meg ⁷ _____ Felix going to make something to eat for the party?
Omri ⁸ _____, he isn't. He's going to buy some crisps and cola.

4 ⭐ **Use the information to write sentences about the people's plans for tonight using *going to*.**

Plans for tonight ...
1 Mel – cook dinner
2 Will and Harry – sing in a concert
3 I – watch Will and Harry
4 Mr Green – look for another job
5 My parents – buy a new camera
6 My sister – phone her boyfriend

Tonight ...
1 *Mel is going to cook dinner.*
2 _____
3 _____
4 _____
5 _____
6 _____

5 ⭐⭐ **Use the information about people's plans for Saturday to correct the sentences.**

Plans for Saturday:
Mel – go shopping
Will and Harry – play tennis
I – stay at home
Mr Green – cook dinner
My parents – drive to the seaside
My sister – meet her boyfriend

1 Mel is going to watch TV.
   She isn't going to watch TV. She's going to go shopping.
2 Will and Harry are going to play football.
   _____
3 I'm going to meet my friends.
   _____
4 Mr Green is going to get a takeaway.
   _____
5 My parents are going to drive to the mountains.
   _____
6 My sister is going to meet her friends.
   _____

6 ★★ Put the words in order to make sentences.

1 to / in May / going / have / trip / we're / a school
We're going to have a school trip in May.

2 going / work / today / you / to / how much / do / are / ?
_____

3 the football / to / going / match / watch / not / tonight / I'm
_____

4 the concert / when / for / tickets / are / buy / going / you / to / ?
_____

5 celebrate / you / to / your / where / birthday / going / are / ?
_____

6 isn't / Helen / to / next / going / year / French / study

7 ★★ Complete the dialogue with the correct forms of the verbs in brackets and *going to*.

Alexa What **1**_are you going to do_ (you/do) this weekend?

Marcy Mum and dad **2**_____ (visit) my aunt but I **3**_____ (not/go) with them. I'm going to stay at home. How about you?

Alexa I **4**_____ (buy) some new clothes with Sheena. Do you want to come with us? We **5**_____ (get) a bus at about 10.30.

Marcy OK, that sounds good. I can buy some food. I **6**_____ (make) a cake for my mum. It's her birthday on Monday.

Alexa Cool. Which supermarket **7**_____ (you/go) to?

Marcy Campbell's. It's the cheapest.

Alexa Great. Sheena and I **8**_____ (start) our shopping trip in HiTime. That's really close to Campbell's. Keep your phone on and call us when you've got what you need.

Marcy OK, see you soon.

8 ★★ Read the answers and use the prompts to write questions with *going to*.

1 go / to the new art gallery later?
Are you going to go to the new art gallery later?
Yes, I am.

2 What / eat / tonight?
_____
My parents are going to eat a pizza tonight.

3 What / watch / this evening?
_____
My dad's going to watch a film.

4 Why / go / to bed early tonight?
_____
I'm going to go to bed early because I'm tired.

5 Who / buy a present for Miss Lane?
_____
Tom's going to buy the present. We all gave him some money for it.

9 ★★★ Complete the dialogue with the correct forms of the verbs from the box and *going to*.

I/ask   I/find   I/not/go   they/go   they/talk   ~~you/do~~
you/go

Gracie Euan, what **1**_are you going to do_ this summer?

Euan **2**_____ a job.

Gracie Really? Where?

Euan I don't know. **3**_____ in shops and restaurants and see what they say. How about you? Have you got any plans?

Gracie Not yet. Margie and Annabella want me to go on holiday with them. **4**_____ camping. They're going to buy a tent this weekend.

Euan Great. **5**_____ with them?

Gracie **6**_____ shopping with them. I haven't got time. I'm not sure about camping. I'd like to go. My parents want to know more about the holiday. **7**_____ to Margie's parents. I hope they say yes.

10 ON A HIGH NOTE Write about your plans for next week using some of the verbs from the lesson.

7B VOCABULARY | Places in the city and transport

1 ⭐ **Match things and activities 1–9 with places a–i.**

1 ☐ paintings   **a** station
2 ☐ money   **b** concert hall
3 ☐ music   **c** library
4 ☐ sleeping   **d** museum
5 ☐ shopping   **e** cinema
6 ☐ exhibition   **f** art gallery
7 ☐ train   **g** hotel
8 ☐ films   **h** market
9 ☐ books   **i** bank

2 ⭐⭐ **Match the words from the box with the definitions.**

bridge   castle   ~~church~~   hospital   park   post office
sports centre   square   supermarket   theatre
tourist information centre

1 It's a religious building. *church*
2 You go there when you're ill. _____
3 It's a good place to take your dog for a walk. _____
4 You go here to buy stamps and to send letters.
_____
5 In this building, you can play sports and keep fit.
_____
6 This is a big shop. You can buy food and things for the house here. _____
7 You can see actors in plays here. _____
8 This is a useful place for holidaymakers. You can get maps and other things here. _____
9 You need this to cross from one side of a river to the other. _____
10 This is an old building. Kings often lived in them.
_____
11 This is an open space in the centre of a town. There are buildings all around it and you can often sit outside a café here in the summer. _____

3 ⭐⭐ **Complete the dialogue with one word in each gap.**

Neil   How can I get to your house?
Molly   ¹B<u>y</u> car!
Neil   I haven't got a car.
Molly   Well, you can ²t_____ the bus to Oak Street.
³G_____ off outside the supermarket.
It's only ten minutes on ⁴f_____ from there
to my house. Phone me when you get there,
and I can come and get you. Then we can
⁵w_____ to my house together.
Neil   Great. What time is the last bus in the evening?
Molly   Don't worry about that. My dad can ⁶d_____
you home in his car.

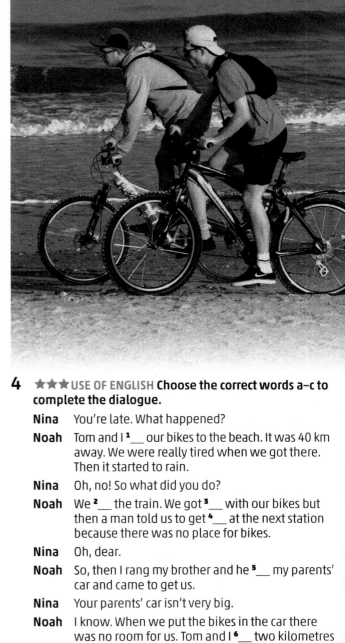

4 ⭐⭐⭐ USE OF ENGLISH **Choose the correct words a–c to complete the dialogue.**

Nina   You're late. What happened?
Noah   Tom and I ¹__ our bikes to the beach. It was 40 km away. We were really tired when we got there. Then it started to rain.
Nina   Oh, no! So what did you do?
Noah   We ²__ the train. We got ³__ with our bikes but then a man told us to get ⁴__ at the next station because there was no place for bikes.
Nina   Oh, dear.
Noah   So, then I rang my brother and he ⁵__ my parents' car and came to get us.
Nina   Your parents' car isn't very big.
Noah   I know. When we put the bikes in the car there was no room for us. Tom and I ⁶__ two kilometres to the bus station and waited for the bus.
Tom took the bus to the stop near the town ⁷__ and I came here ⁸__ foot. Now I need a warm drink and some food.

1 **a** drove   **b** rode   **c** got
2 **a** took   **b** drove   **c** rode
3 **a** through   **b** up   **c** on
4 **a** down   **b** away   **c** off
5 **a** rode   **b** drove   **c** went
6 **a** walked   **b** arrived   **c** got
7 **a** hall   **b** house   **c** home
8 **a** with   **b** on   **c** in

5 ON A HIGH NOTE **Write about how you get from your home to different places in your town, e.g. school, the town centre, friends' houses, the railway station.**

UNIT VOCABULARY PRACTICE > page 85

7C LISTENING

1 🔊 *49* **Where are the speakers? Listen to messages 1–5 and match them with places a–g. There are two extra places.**

☐ Message 1   **a** an airport
☐ Message 2   **b** a concert hall
☐ Message 3   **c** a cinema
☐ Message 4   **d** a ferry
☐ Message 5   **e** a car park
              f a different country
              g a train station

2 🔊 *49* **Listen to the messages again and choose the correct answers.**

1 What problem did the speaker and his father have?
   a The car park closed for the night before they left.
   b It took a long time to do their shopping.
   c They couldn't drive away because of a different car.

2 What do we know about the speaker?
   a She didn't have any popcorn during the first film.
   b She's going to stay at the cinema all night.
   c She fell asleep during the first film.

3 What is the third speaker's main message?
   a Their flight was delayed.
   b Their journey is going well.
   c They are now safely at their holiday destination.

4 What did the speaker NOT like on the ferry?
   a The time of the announcement.
   b The food offered at breakfast.
   c The room she slept in.

5 What new information does the speaker mention in his message?
   a What time the concert starts.
   b Where they arranged to meet.
   c Where his friend can collect her ticket.

Vocabulary extension

3 🔊 *50* **Complete the extracts from the recording in Exercise 1 with the words from the box. Listen and check.**

check-in   ferry   ~~marathon~~   miss   on

1 The film *marathon* started at midnight and is going to last for nine hours.
2 The train was _____ time.
3 I took my suitcase to the _____ counter.
4 I really enjoyed travelling by _____!
5 I don't want to _____ my favourite band.

4 ON A HIGH NOTE **Imagine you're late to meet your friend. Write a text message to explain where you are, why you are late and what you are going to do.**

Pronunciation

ACTIVE PRONUNCIATION | /æ/ and /eɪ/ sounds

When we add the letter *e* to the end of a one-syllable word which has the letter *a*, the pronunciation changes:
hat /'hæt/ – *hate* /'heɪt/
mad /'mæd/ – *made* /'meɪd/

5 🔊 *51* **Find one word with the /æ/ sound and one word with the /eɪ/ sound in each of these sentences. Listen and repeat.**

1 Hi Sam, I'm going to be a bit late.
2 Hi Max, it's a shame you aren't here.
3 I met an old schoolmate so I sat with her.
4 I'm drinking a can of cola and eating a cake.
5 Dad went but I hate getting up early.

6 🔊 *52* **Say hi to these people. Be careful when you pronounce their names. Listen, check and repeat.**

1 Hi, Sam!
2 Hi, Jane!
3 Hi, Jack!
4 Hi, Jake!
5 Hi, Dave!
6 Hi, Max!

7 🔊 *53* **Listen and tick the word you hear.**

I hate this hat.

1 ☑ hat   ☐ hate
2 ☐ mad   ☐ made
3 ☐ tap   ☐ tape
4 ☐ plan   ☐ plane
5 ☐ back   ☐ bake
6 ☐ at   ☐ ate
7 ☐ Max   ☐ makes
8 ☐ cat   ☐ Kate

7D GRAMMAR

Present Continuous: future arrangements

1 ★ Complete the mini-conversations with the Present Continuous forms of the verbs in brackets.

A

Viola I can't make it to your party, I'm afraid. It's my mum's birthday and we **1** *'re going* (go) to a restaurant.

Roxette That's a shame. Connor **2**_____ (come). He phoned earlier. He's back from his holidays.

B

Kylie What **3**_____ (you/do) this afternoon?

Josh I **4**_____ (meet) Adrian at four o'clock. We **5**_____ (get) a present for Simon's birthday.

C

James Why **6**_____ (you/not play) football after school today?

Andrea I can't. I **7**_____ (go) to the dentist at five o'clock.

D

Luke **8**_____ (you/go) out this evening?

Karen Yes, I am. I **9**_____ (go) to the cinema with Rose. We **10**_____ (meet) at 6 p.m.

2 ★★ Complete the intentions with the verbs from the box and the correct forms of *going to*. Then match the sentences with the mini-conversations from Exercise 1.

~~buy~~ eat play show

1 ☐ We *'re going to buy* him some special pens from the art shop.

2 ☐ We _____ something before the film starts – maybe a pizza.

3 ☐ He _____ us his photos from India.

4 ☐ But I _____ tomorrow.

3 ★★★ Look at the diary and complete the sentences using the Present Continuous and *going to*.

Monday	Meeting with Mr Bishop about the Maths competition – 10 a.m.
	Meet Jane at Allie's Coffee Bar – 3 p.m.
Tuesday	HOLIDAYS START!
	Tennis with Alison – 10 a.m. (Play better this time!)
	Meet Ray – 4.30 p.m.
Wednesday	Dentist – 9.a.m., ask about broken tooth.
	Party at home, 8 guests – 7 p.m.: make some cool snacks.
Friday	Jaqui arriving by train 1.45 p.m., meet her at the station, show her the town.
	A chance to practise my French!

1 I *'m meeting Mr Bishop about the Maths competition* at 10 a.m. on Monday.

2 I _____ at Allie's Coffee Bar on Monday afternoon.

3 I _____ with Alison on Tuesday morning.

4 I _____ better this time!

5 Ray and I _____ 4.30 p.m on Tuesday.

6 I _____ on Wednesday morning.

7 I _____ about my broken tooth.

8 Eight people _____ at my house on Wednesday!

9 I _____ some cool snacks for the party.

10 I _____ at 1.45 p.m. at the train station.

11 I _____ the town.

12 I _____ my French!

4 ★★★ Complete the questions about the diary in Exercise 3.

1 *When are you meeting* Mr Bishop?
At 10 a.m. on Monday.

2 _____ Jane?
At Allie's Coffee Bar.

3 _____ on Tuesday afternoon?
Ray.

4 _____ the dentist?
Because I've got a broken tooth.

5 _____ the party?
Eight.

6 _____ Jaqui?
At 1.45 p.m.

5 ON A HIGH NOTE Write about some definite arrangements you, or people you know, have for the next week.

1 🔊 54 Listen and repeat the phrases. How do you say them in your language?

SPEAKING | Asking for and giving directions

ASKING FOR DIRECTIONS

Excuse me/Sorry, where's the railway station?

Where's Blackwall station?

How do I get to Blackwall station?

Can you tell me the way to the station?

Where's the nearest post office?

Is there a visitor information centre **near here?**

GIVING DIRECTIONS

Go/Walk to the end of Queen Street.

Go/Walk straight on.

Take the first/second road on the left/right.

Go/Walk along Green Street.

Turn left/right at the traffic lights.

Go/Walk past the library.

It's on the left/right.

It's opposite/next to a supermarket.

2 Match sentences 1–6 with pictures A–F.

1. ☐ Go past the café.
2. ☐ It's opposite the café.
3. ☐ It's next to a café.
4. ☐ Walk to the end of the road.
5. ☐ Take the second road on the left.
6. ☐ Walk straight on.

3 🔊 55 Complete the dialogue with one word in each gap. Listen and check.

Sandra ¹E*xcuse* me, can you tell me ²w_____ the Royal English School is, please?

Man Royal English School? Do you know which street it's in?

Sandra Yes, the address is 45A Surrey Lane.

Man Oh, right. Go ³a_____ this road for 400 metres. When you come to the end of the road, turn ⁴r_____. That's Nelson Road. Then ⁵t_____ the second turning on the left. That's Green Lane. Go ⁶p_____ the bank and the post office. Just after the post office there's a school. ⁷O_____ the school is a park. Walk through the park and on the other side is Surrey Lane.

Sandra Oh, dear. It's very complicated.

Man Well, don't worry. There's a bus stop just here, ⁸n_____ to the car park. You can take the number 49. It goes to Surrey Lane. Just ask the driver to tell you when to get off.

Sandra OK. Oh, here comes the bus now. Thank you very much. Bye.

4 Complete the mini-conversations with one word in each gap.

Andrea Excuse ¹*me*. Where's the railway station?

Man Walk straight ²_____ for about 200 metres.

Sally Where's ³_____ nearest bank?

Woman It's about 400 metres from here. Walk to the ⁴_____ of King Street and turn left at the traffic lights.

Noah Is ⁵_____ a cinema near here?

Man Yes. ⁶_____ the first road on the left and it's on the right.

Andrew How do I ⁷_____ to Baker Street?

Woman Walk ⁸_____ Regent Street. Go past the supermarket and turn righ. That's Baker Street.

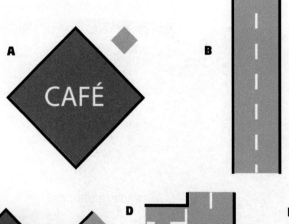

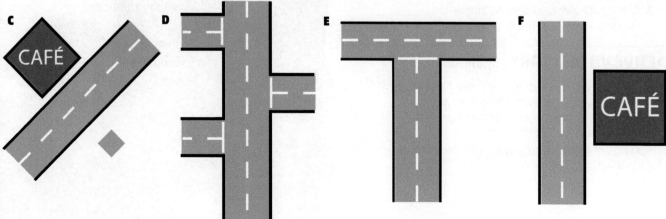

7F READING AND VOCABULARY

1 Read the text quickly and match paragraphs 1–4 with photos A–D.

Paragraph 1 ☐   Paragraph 3 ☐

Paragraph 2 ☐   Paragraph 4 ☐

2 Read the text again and match teenagers A–E with paragraphs 1–4. There is one extra person.

A ☐ Ellie wants an activity that will let her explore the town during the day.

B ☐ Tom wants to meet other people his own age and do an activity in an art gallery.

C ☐ Jack and his friends enjoy looking at interesting exhibitions but are busy during the daytime.

D ☐ Celina wants to have an interesting time in the evening and get some exercise.

E ☐ Rosie loves doing activities with other people and solving puzzles.

Vocabulary extension

3 Find the words in the text that match these definitions.

1 Twelve o'clock at night. (intro) m_idnight_

2 A competition, party, concert or other activity which people take part in or watch. (para 1) e_____

3 Something you want to do and achieve in the future. (para 2) a_____

4 Something strange that is difficult to understand or explain. (para 2) m_____

5 A number of things you write on a piece of paper. It may be things you have to do or things you have to buy. (para 3) l_____

6 A person who joins a club becomes one. (para 4) m_____

4 Complete the sentences with the words from Exercise 3.

1 I had a lot of homework to do and it was _midnight_ when I went to bed.

2 I'm at the supermarket but I haven't got the shopping _____. Do we need milk?

3 My _____ is to get into the school football team this year.

4 I'm sorry, you can't come into this club. You aren't a _____.

5 I still don't know who this letter is from. It's a _____.

6 Our school always organises interesting _____ for new students at the beginning of the school year.

ACTIVE VOCABULARY | Synonyms

Synonyms are words which have the same meaning. They can be verbs, adjectives, adverbs or nouns (e.g. *find out – discover, big – large, quickly – fast, teams – groups*).

When you are writing, don't repeat the same words. Use synonyms.

---

5 Match words from the text 1–8 with their synonyms a–h.

1 ☐ maybe   **a** only

2 ☐ let us know   **b** mum and dad

3 ☐ just   **c** perhaps

4 ☐ great   **d** end

5 ☐ unusual   **e** kind

6 ☐ sort   **f** tell us

7 ☐ parents   **g** strange

8 ☐ finish   **h** wonderful

6 Replace the underlined words in the sentences below with the correct forms of the synonyms from Exercise 5.

1 We saw an unusual light and heard <u>an unusual</u> sound. _a strange_

2 The hotel was great and the food was <u>great</u>. _____

3 The show <u>finished</u> when the last song finished. _____

4 Tell us what time you will arrive and <u>tell us</u> what you want to eat. _____

5 I'm going on holiday with my parents. I like spending time with my <u>parents</u>. _____

6 We <u>just</u> have half an hour but, don't worry, we don't have to answer every question, just three of them. _____

7 Maybe it was a dream or <u>maybe</u> I saw it in a film. _____

8 It's a sort of sightseeing tour with a <u>sort</u> of show at the end of it. _____

7 ON A HIGH NOTE Write about an interesting or unusual activity that you can do in your town or country.

UNIT VOCABULARY PRACTICE > page 85

What's on in your town?

07

Teenagers often complain that there is nothing to do. Here are some teenagers who are lucky to live in towns where people organise activities that they can enjoy. Maybe your town also runs similar events. If so, let us know.

1 Night at the museum

This year, on June 10th, the museums in our town are going to stay open all night, not just until midnight. You can look round the museum as usual or take part in one of the organised events. Among other things, there's going to be a 'treasure hunt'. You have to find specific things in the museum. It isn't a competition, but it feels good to find all the items. I like that sort of thing – it makes you look more carefully at the things on display. *Alice*

2 Murder Mystery at the library

I'm taking part in the Murder Mystery evening on Friday. This is the third murder mystery in our library and the aim is to encourage teenagers to read more and find out about the books in the library. To find the answers to the clues, you have to read different books. Not the whole book! Just a page or two. You work in teams and the winning team is the one that discovers who the murderer is first. *Ben*

3 Photo Hunt

I love photography so this is a great idea for me. You get a list of twenty things you must photograph in the city. Last year one of the items was 'a picture of a red man'. I spent an hour in the art gallery, but I couldn't find a painting or sculpture of a red man. When the competition finished, you could see the winners' photos online. The red man was on a light for crossing the road! This year I'm going to take my bike and work in a group with some friends. Together, we can win! *Connor*

4 Night riders

Our local cycling club organises a night ride on Friday evenings. I'm not a member of the club but my parents are. They go every week, but I go about once a month because I'm often busy on Fridays. This week, some of my friends are going to come with me. We cycle round and watch out for interesting or unusual sights. There are lots of cycle paths so it's very safe. Then we all stop at a café in the town square. It's very relaxing and healthy. *Debbie*

83

7G WRITING | A short message

Start the message appropriately.

Leave out *to be* and subject pronoun *I* where possible.

Leave out conjunctions where possible.

Leave out articles.

Finish the message appropriately.

> Mum,
>
> ¹_____ At Josie's. We're doing a project together. Back at about 8 p.m. ²_____ Eating there – you don't need to worry about dinner for me. Josie's parents invited me. ³_____ Hope it's OK.
>
> ⁴_____ Letter from school on ⁵_____ table. Please read and sign ⁶_____ so I can take it tomorrow.
>
> See you later,
>
> Natalie

1 Read the message and choose the correct answer.
Natalie
a wants her mum to write a letter to her school.
b doesn't need any food at home.
c wants to invite a friend to her house.

2 Match the words below, which were left out in the message in Exercise 1, with gaps 1–6.
☐ I'm ☐ it
☐ I ☐ There's a
☐ the ☐ I'm

3 Imagine each sentence is a part of a different short message. Find any unnecessary words.
1 ~~I'm~~ going to try to get ~~some~~ tickets for ~~the~~ concert later.
2 There is some money for you on the kitchen cupboard.
3 We're going to be late home because the train is late.
4 There is some food in the fridge. You just need to warm it up.
5 The bus stops outside the bank. I'll meet you there.

4 In messages to older family members or people we don't know very well, we don't usually miss out words. Complete the message with the words from the box.

I (x2) I'm (x2) I've the

> Hi Juan,
> ¹I hope you're OK. ²_____ got my ticket to Spain.
> ³_____ arriving at Madrid Airport on Saturday, July 20ᵗʰ at 6.45 p.m. My flight number is ER 7123.
> ⁴_____ very happy that your parents can come to the airport to pick me up. My parents are happy too!
> I know it isn't difficult to get the train but ⁵_____ was still a bit nervous about travelling on my own.
> It'll be great to see you at ⁶_____ airport.
> I'll try to learn some Spanish before I arrive.
> See you soon,
> Aaron

5 WRITING TASK Write two messages.
A Write a reply from Juan to the email in Exercise 4. Thank Aaron for sending the information and tell him about some interesting activities you plan to do while he's staying with you.
B Aaron is now in Madrid. He arrived yesterday. Write a text message from Aaron to his friend in England saying where he is and what he's doing.

ACTIVE WRITING | A short message
1 Plan your messages.
• Think of the messages you want to write.
• Make notes about the information you want to include.
2 Write the messages.
• Start by writing the two messages in full.
• Make sure the style of the language is suitable for the person you are writing to.
• For the text message, decide which words you can leave out. Rewrite this note in its short form.
3 Check that ...
• you have included all the relevant information.
• there are no spelling or grammar mistakes.

UNIT VOCABULARY PRACTICE

1 7A GRAMMAR AND VOCABULARY **Match the two parts of the phrases.**

Next year, I'm going to …

1 ☐ visit   **a** to my cousin's 21st birthday party.
2 ☐ stay   **b** a barbecue for my birthday.
3 ☐ book   **c** some interesting museums.
4 ☐ have   **d** a summer job.
5 ☐ get   **e** tickets for some great concerts.
6 ☐ go   **f** at home all summer.

2 7B VOCABULARY **Complete the text with the words from the box.**

bridge   gallery   hall   hotel   ~~information~~   office
park   square

Woman Hello, welcome to the Tourist ¹*Information* Centre. How can I help you?

Annie I'd like a city map, please.

Woman Here you are. This is a good size for tourists. Which ²_____ are you staying in?

Annie The Grand.

Woman Ah, yes. Next to the National Art ³_____. That's here. You cross the river on this very old ⁴_____.

Annie Yes, we did that this morning.

Woman Then you come to King Street. It's the main street in the town. There are lots of shops, there's a post ⁵_____ and the new concert ⁶_____. At the end of the street there is a beautiful ⁷_____ where you can relax in peace and quiet. It's also a great place to walk, cycle or play sports.

Annie Where's the best place to eat?

Woman There are lots of good restaurants in the main ⁸_____ of the town. It's a beautiful place and it's always busy. My favourite restaurant is La Casa del Abuelo. The food is delicious.

3 7B VOCABULARY **Complete the sentences with one word in each gap.**

1 Do you want to t*ake* the bus or go on f_____?
2 Don't r_____ a bike in the city centre. It's too dangerous.
3 I think we should go to the airport b_____ taxi.
4 We're going to Italy this summer. Dad wants to d_____ our car, but mum wants to go by plane.
5 When you arrive at the train s_____, go outside and find the bus stop. Get o_____ bus 175 and, after 10 minutes, get o_____ at the university.

4 7F READING AND VOCABULARY **Choose the correct words to complete the sentences.**

1 We should __ the timetable online. Sometimes there are changes.
   a check   **b** book   **c** take
2 You can __ your ticket online. You don't need to go to the travel agency.
   a hire   **b** buy   **c** find
3 If you __ a place on the same flight as me, my parents can take you to the airport.
   a stay   **b** book   **c** take
4 I think the best way to learn a foreign language is to __ with a host family.
   a book   **b** stay   **c** meet
5 The hotel says we can __ bikes from them for 10 euros a day or 40 euros for the whole week.
   a hire   **b** take   **c** buy
6 Don't worry about looking for hotels now. It's easy to __ accommodation in September.
   a buy   **b** stay   **c** find
7 We can __ a tour on our first day to see the city and find out something about it.
   a hire   **b** buy   **c** take
8 My friends are preparing for their exams, so this summer I'm going to the camp __ my own.
   a on   **b** at   **c** with

5 ON A HIGH NOTE **Write about a new place you would like to see in your town. Explain why you think your town needs this place.**

1 **For each learning objective, write 1–5 to assess your ability.**

1 = I don't feel confident. 5 = I feel confident.

	Learning objective	Course material	How confident I am (1–5)
7A	I can use *going to* and the Present Continuous to talk about future intentions and plans.	Student's Book pp. 90–91 Workbook pp. 76–77	
7B	I can talk about places and transport in cities.	Student's Book p. 92 Workbook p. 78	
7C	I can understand new words in announcements.	Student's Book p. 93 Workbook p. 79	
7D	I can use the Present Continuous to talk about future plans and arrangements.	Student's Book p. 94 Workbook p. 80	
7E	I can ask for and give directions.	Student's Book p. 95 Workbook p. 81	
7F	I can identify specific information in online forum posts and talk about travelling.	Student's Book pp. 96–97 Workbook pp. 82–83	
7G	I can write a short message.	Student's Book p. 98 Workbook p. 84	

2 **Which of the skills above would you like to improve in? How?**

Skill I want to improve in	How I can improve

3 **What can you remember from this unit?**

New words I learned and most want to remember	Expressions and phrases I liked	English I heard or read outside class

Self-check

GRAMMAR AND VOCABULARY

1 Complete the phrases with one word in each gap to replace the underlined parts of the sentences.

1 When I go to France, I want to <u>travel to</u> the Palace of Versailles. t__ake__ a t__rip__ to see
2 I'm going to <u>work this summer</u>. g_____ a summer j_____.
3 We're going to London to <u>look at the famous buildings</u>. d_____ some s_____.
4 Do you want to <u>eat something</u> at our house? h_____ a m_____.
5 Look at the <u>information about trains and when they leave and arrive</u>. t_____ t_____.
6 You need to look hard <u>for somewhere to stay</u> here in the summer. to f_____ a_____.

/ 5

2 Complete the sentences with one word in each gap.

1 It's sunny today. We can go <u>to</u> the beach.
2 The best way to get to the seaside is to go _____ train.
3 I hate it when people try to get _____ the bus before I have a chance to get off.
4 You can't leave the car in the street. There's a car _____ near here which has got lots of space.
5 It isn't easy getting _____ the metro. People start getting on before you can leave the train.
6 This is a big city. We can't see everything _____ foot. We need to use the metro too.

/ 5

3 Use *going to* and the prompts to complete the sentences.

1 *What are you going to do* (What/you/do) tonight?
2 I don't feel well. _____ (I/not/do) any work this evening.
3 Jason doesn't want to go out on Saturday. _____ (he/spend) the day listening to his new CDs.
4 Do you want to come to the town centre with us? _____ (We/get) a pizza.
5 _____ (your parents/bring) you something nice from the USA?
6 Don't buy a takeaway tomorrow. _____ (Elle/cook) something nice for us.

/ 5

4 Use the notes to write sentences in the Present Continuous and *going to*.

Friday 12ᵗʰ March

1 look for a new dress
2 meet Chloe at 10 a.m.
3 Chloe – buy some new shoes

Saturday 13ᵗʰ March

4 Chloe – go to a party with her boyfriend
5 My cousins – come for my dad's birthday
6 My brother and I – make him a cake

1 *I'm going to look for a new dress on Friday.*
2 _____
3 _____
4 _____
5 _____
6 _____

/ 5

USE OF ENGLISH

5 Choose the correct answers a–c to complete the sentences.

1 When the ___ office is closed, you can buy stamps here.

  a town   **b** post   **c** train

2 With our app it is easier to ___ a place on a tour.

  a catch   **b** book   **c** take

3 Please wait here to ___ the plane. Have your tickets and passports ready.

  a travel   **b** drive   **c** board

4 You can ___ a barbecue in the garden but please don't play loud music after 10 p.m.

  a take   **b** have   **c** visit

5 Please do NOT ___ bikes in the park.

  a ride   **b** drive   **c** travel

/ 5

6 Complete the second sentence using the word in bold so that it means the same as the first one. Use no more than three words including the word in bold.

1 We're going to watch a film this evening. **GO**
  We're going *to go to* the cinema this evening.
2 My accommodation is going to be in a family's house. **HOST**
  I'm going to stay _____ family.
3 I'm going to pay for my flight online. **PLANE**
  I'm going to buy _____ online.
4 My plan is to finish this book this weekend. **GOING**
  I _____ finish this book this weekend.
5 We can take the bus tomorrow. **BY**
  We can _____ tomorrow.
6 What are your parents' holiday plans for the summer? **GO**
  Where are your parents _____ this summer?

/ 5

/ 30

08 Smart future

8A GRAMMAR AND VOCABULARY

Will

1 ★ Complete the text with *will* or *won't*.

Will you have a drone in the future?

Comments

No, people ¹*won't* have drones because they are dangerous. There was a problem in the UK once when a drone flew near an airport and all the flights stopped. Soon, there ²_____ be an accident and the government ³_____ say that only companies and people like the police and army can have drones. ***Josh***

Yes, I ⁴_____ take it on holiday so that I can take great photos. I think schools ⁵_____ tell students not to bring drones to school but they ⁶_____ be great fun in your free time. I ⁷_____ make films with my drone but I ⁸_____ do anything dangerous like flying it near roads. That's wrong. ***Natalie***

2 ★★ Complete the sentences with *will* or *won't* and the correct verbs from the box.

~~be~~ buy drive eat go have spend use

By 2050 ...
1. there *won't be* any traditional TV channels. ✗
2. we _____ money to buy things. ✗
3. people _____ on virtual holidays. ✓
4. people _____ meat. ✗
5. we _____ everything on the Internet. ✓
6. people _____ cars. ✗
7. people _____ their free time on '20ᵗʰ century, technology-free' holidays. ✓
8. students _____ teachers. ✗

3 ★★ Put the words in order to make sentences.

Are you optimistic or pessimistic about the future? Here is what some of my friends say.

Optimistic friends

1. have / technology / will / of / easier / because / we / lives
   We will have easier lives because of technology.
2. longer / will / live / we
   _____
3. clean / will / energy / scientists / of / find / forms / new
   _____
4. help / people / each / other / will
   _____

Pessimistic friends

5. the / few / world / control / a / will / companies / big
   _____
6. world / hotter / the / get / will
   _____
7. the time / will / us / watch / all / governments
   _____

What do you think?

4 ★★ Read the questions and write short answers.
In the future ...
1. will the world be cleaner?
   ✓ *Yes, it will.*
2. will we live longer?
   ✓ _____
3. will we be able to see other people's thoughts?
   ✗ _____
4. will we have technology under our skin?
   ✓ _____
5. will America be the most powerful country?
   ✗ _____
6. will people be happier than they are now?
   ✗ _____

5 ★★ Complete the sentences using *will* and the words in brackets.

1 Next year *I will be able to drive* (I/can/drive).
2 In 50 years, _____ (we/can/fly) to Australia in two hours.
3 In 10 years, _____ (people/can/go) on holiday to space.
4 In four years time, _____ (I/can/watch) any film I like.
5 Get a passport! _____ (you/can/travel) to other countries.
6 Get a special cover for your phone. _____ (you/can/take) photos underwater.
7 This language app is great. In one year _____ (I/can/speak) French.

6 ★★ Complete the mini-conversations using *will*.

Ann What job ¹*will you have* in the future?
Sam I'm not sure. I'd like to be a doctor.

Paul Where ² _____ in the future?
Vicky In the future, I will live in the USA.

Noah ³ _____ rich?
Andrea I hope so. I want to live in a big house and not worry about money!

Aaron What ⁴ _____ in your free time?
Emma I'll do lots of sports and exercise.

Sarah Where ⁵ _____ on your holidays?
Sally All over the world.

Michael ⁶ _____ any pets?
Robert No, I won't.

7 ★★★ Complete the second sentence using *will/won't be able to* and the verb in bold.

1 At the moment doctors can't help people with some diseases. **CURE**
By 2100, doctors *will be able to cure* all diseases.
2 Students can now do some homework online. **TAKE**
By 2030, students _____ exams online.
3 We can watch films, read books and listen to music for free online. **USE**
In the future, we _____ the Internet for free. We will have to pay for it.
4 We can book flights and hotels online. **TRAVEL**
In the future, we _____ all over the world using Virtual Reality.
5 The police can use security cameras to help them find criminals. **HIDE**
Criminals _____ from the police because there will be cameras watching us everywhere.
6 We can use apps to check our health. **SWITCH OFF**
In the future, we _____ these apps. Doctors will watch them all the time and send us messages – 'Do more exercise! Go to bed earlier!'

8 ★★★ USE OF ENGLISH Complete the text with one word in each gap.

CAN YOU PREDICT THE FUTURE?

Although it's difficult to predict the future, people like to try. Here are some ideas but ¹*will they come true?*

Deserts will become tropical forests. We can already see 'desert greening' in some places but this will ² _____ happen quickly. Perhaps ³ _____ one thousand years there will be green deserts.

What about countries? Will maps look the same as they do now? ⁴ _____ will almost certainly be some changes. Some people think that, ⁵ _____ the year 2050, California will be an independent country. Will it be ⁶ _____ to survive as a country on its own? The simple answer is 'Yes'. Only four countries in the world are richer than California: The USA, China, Japan and Germany.

What about a prediction for the ⁷ _____ few years? Will an astronaut get to Mars? Will the world keep getting hotter? What do you think?

9 ON A HIGH NOTE Write five predictions about the future. Think about the world, your country, your town, your life.

8B VOCABULARY | Computer equipment

1 ★ Complete the crossword with verbs (v) or nouns (n).

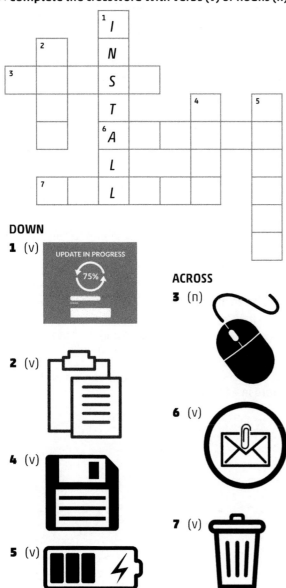

DOWN

1 (v) UPDATE IN PROGRESS 75%

2 (v)

4 (v)

5 (v)

ACROSS

3 (n)

6 (v)

7 (v)

2 ★★ Complete the sentences with the words from the box.

~~battery~~ cable desktop disk screens speakers wireless

1 This laptop _battery_ is very old. It lasts for half an hour.
2 You can connect your phone to your laptop using a USB _____. It's very easy.
3 My parents still have an old _____ computer. It's very heavy and slow.
4 You spend all day looking at _____– on your phone, your laptop and the TV.
5 The computer has a 1TB hard _____ so I can keep lots of films and songs on it.
6 A _____ mouse is good – you can move it easily.
7 My laptop doesn't have very good sound, so I connect _____ to it to listen to music.

3 ★★ Complete the dialogue with one verb in each gap.

Adrian You look busy.

Pablo I am. Every time I switch on my computer, someone in my family asks me to do something for them.

Adrian Like what?

Pablo Well, my grandmother wants me to ¹_scan_ some old photos and ²s_____ them onto her tablet. My dad wants me to ³p_____ a form for him so he can fill it in and send it to the tax office. He could fill it in online, but he prefers using a pen.

Adrian And ...?

Pablo And my sister wants me to ⁴t_____ a story she wrote. She says I'm quicker than her on a keyboard, which is correct, but it's really difficult to read her writing.

Adrian Oh, dear.

Pablo Oh, and my brother wants me to ⁵d_____ some songs for him for a party.

Adrian And what about your mum? What does she want you to do?

Pablo She wants me to ⁶s_____ o_____ my computer because she says I use it too much!

4 ★★★ USE OF ENGLISH Complete the second sentence using the word in bold so that it means the same as the first one. Use no more than three words including the word in bold.

1 I need to give my battery more energy so that I can use my phone when I go out. **CHARGE**

   I need to _charge my phone_ so I can use it when I go out.

2 Could you make the volume louder, please? I can't hear it. **UP**

   Could you _____ the volume, please? I can't hear it.

3 How much room have you got to store films and other things on your laptop? **DISK**

   How big is _____ on your laptop?

4 Don't leave your computer on all night – it's a waste of energy. **OFF**

   Don't forget to _____ computer at night so that you don't waste energy.

5 You don't need a cable when you use a wireless keyboard. **TO**

   You don't _____ a wireless keyboard to your computer with a cable.

6 It's easy to get new apps and put them onto your phone. **INSTALL**

   It's easy to _____ on your phone.

5 ON A HIGH NOTE Describe your computer or other device using the words from the lesson.

UNIT VOCABULARY PRACTICE > page 97

Adverbs of manner

1 ⭐ **Choose the correct words to complete the sentences. Sometimes more than one answer is possible.**

1 My dad drives very *carefully / fast / healthily*.

2 This computer works *slowly / politely / well*.

3 Our teacher sometimes shouts at us *loudly / hard / safely*.

4 Check your work *politely / carefully / badly*.

5 I ran very *fast / quickly / politely* to the bus stop.

6 The children played *urgently / happily / loudly* together.

7 We all worked *hard / healthily / well* during the lesson.

8 I need to phone home *urgently / dangerously / well*.

2 ⭐⭐ **Complete the text with the correct forms of the words in brackets.**

I bought a new laptop this morning.

I carried it home ²*carefully* (careful). When I got to my bedroom, I opened the box and read the instructions ²_____ (quick) and then switched it on. The laptop started working very ³_____ (quiet). I followed the on-screen instructions ⁴_____ (confident) and went online. Webpages opened very ⁵_____ (fast) and I looked at my social media pages and watched videos ⁶_____ (happy). After an hour, I switched the laptop off ⁷_____ (safe) and put it away in its bag. 'Well,' I thought to myself, 'my brother isn't going to use this, even if he asks really ⁸_____ (polite).' Just then there was a knock on my bedroom door. It was Justin. 'I hear you've got a new laptop,' he said, 'Can I ...?' 'No!' I replied ⁹_____ (loud) and ¹⁰_____ (clear). After he left, I looked ¹¹_____ (slow) round the room thinking about the best place to hide the computer.

3 ⭐⭐ **Complete the sentences with the adjectives in bold and adverbs formed from them.**

1 CAREFUL

Be *careful* when you drive. Drive *carefully*.

2 LOUD

Everyone is talking _____. It's so _____ I can't think!

3 HARD

I work _____ every day. I'm a _____ worker!

4 GOOD

They're a _____ team. They always play very _____.

5 BAD

I had a _____ day. Everything went _____.

6 FAST

This is a _____ car, but you can't drive it _____ on these roads.

7 HEALTHY

I try to eat _____. I always eat _____ food.

4 ⭐⭐⭐ **Complete the mini-conversations with the words from the box. There is one extra word.**

badly carefully hard ~~loud~~ loudly polite politely
slow slowly

Moussa Have you got any speakers? The sound on your laptop isn't very ¹*loud*.

Hassan It is but I can't play music ²_____. My dad works at night and he's sleeping.

Moussa Oh, OK.

Jade Hurry up!

Cheryl I'm ready!

Jade You're so ³_____!

Cheryl I'm not.

Jade You are! You do everything ⁴_____ and you're always late!

Mum Your teacher says you always work ⁵_____ during the lessons.

James I do!

Mum And he says that you're very ⁶_____.

James ... but?

Mum But you did very ⁷_____ in your exams.

James I know.

Mum You made some silly mistakes. He says you should always check your work ⁸_____ when you finish.

James I will, don't worry.

5 ON A HIGH NOTE **Write about how you do different activities. Which do you do well, badly, slowly, carefully, etc.?**

1 🔊 **56 Listen and number the pictures.**

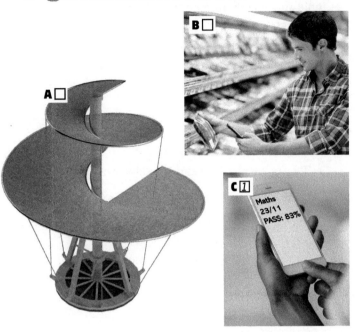

2 🔊 **56 Listen to the conversations again and choose the correct answers.**

1 Two friends talk about an e-register. What are they both worried about?

a Their teacher – he's angry when students are late.

b Their parents when they see their grades.

c A punishment one of them will get for being late.

2 Two friends talk about Leonardo da Vinci. What do you learn about him?

a One of his inventions didn't work when he built it.

b He didn't test any of his inventions.

c His inventions were useful during wars.

3 Two people talk about a new idea at school. What do we know about the idea?

a The teachers and students disagree about the idea.

b Not all the students at the school are trying the idea.

c The students are going to try the idea for a month.

4 What are the people in the shop going to ask about?

a What happens if you take something without paying?

b What happens if you haven't got the money in your bank to pay for the items you buy?

c What happens if you don't like using new technology when you go shopping?

Vocabulary extension

3 🔊 **57 Complete the sentences with the words from the box which you heard in the recording in Exercise 1. Listen and check.**

keen ~~late~~ pleased right upset

1 I don't want to be *late* for my lesson. I must hurry up.

2 I didn't want to go to the party at first but I'm _____ that my friends took me because I enjoyed it.

3 My friend went online to show us all that his answers to the French homework were _____.

4 Some students are _____ because we can't use our phones at school – not even during the breaks.

5 People who aren't _____ on technology don't like using smartphones to pay for things in shops.

4 ON A HIGH NOTE **Think of new technology at school, at home or in your town. Explain what the new idea is and what you think of it.**

Pronunciation

> ### ACTIVE PRONUNCIATION | Stress in compound nouns
>
> Compound nouns are words created from two nouns or an adjective and a noun (e.g. *bathroom*, *greenhouse*).
>
> In compound nouns, we put the stress on the first word (e.g. **bath**room).

5 🔊 **58 Listen to four sentences from the recording in Exercise 1. Write the compound nouns. Tick the one which is formed with an adjective and a noun.**

1 ☐ *smartphone*   **3** ☐ _____

2 ☐ _____   **4** ☐ _____

6 🔊 **59 Listen to the words from Exercise 5 and repeat them with the correct stress.**

7 🔊 **60 Complete the compound nouns with the words from the box. Listen, check and repeat.**

board end mate phones place table ~~track~~ washer

1 sound*track*   **5** dish_____

2 head_____   **6** room_____

3 week_____   **7** skate_____

4 fire_____   **8** time_____

8 🔊 **61 Listen and write the words. Then listen and repeat.**

1 s*upermarket*

2 c_____ _____k

3 h_____k

4 t_____t

5 k_____d

6 s_____h

1 🔊 62 Listen and repeat the phrases. How do you say them in your language?

SPEAKING | Opinions

GIVING OPINIONS

(Personally,) I think that tablets are more useful than laptops.

(Personally,) I don't think that a wireless mouse is very useful.

In my opinion, you use your phone too much.

I'm sure that we'll do all our lessons on tablets in the future.

AGREEING

Yes, I agree.

You're right.

Exactly.

I agree with him/her/you.

I think so too.

DISAGREEING

(I'm sorry but) I don't agree.

That's (probably) true but I still prefer my old laptop.

I'm not sure (about that).

I don't think so.

2 Read and choose A for agreeing, D for disagreeing or O for giving opinions.

1 I agree. A / D / O
2 I don't think so. A / D / O
3 Personally, I think that under 16's shouldn't use social media. A / D / O
4 I'm not sure about that. A / D / O
5 In my opinion, Chinese is more important than French. A / D / O
6 You're right. A / D / O
7 I'm sure that a new form of social media will take over the Internet soon. A / D / O
8 I think so too. A / D / O
9 I'm sorry but I don't agree. A / D / O

3 Read the initial sentence and match the two parts of the possible responses.

In my opinion, we shouldn't have homework during the holidays because this is a time when we should relax.

1 ☐ I think   a you.
2 ☐ I'm sorry but I   b so too.
3 ☐ Yes, I   c true but I still don't think
4 ☐ I'm not   our teachers will agree.
5 ☐ You're   d don't agree.
6 ☐ I agree with   e right.
7 ☐ That's probably   f sure about that.
                 g agree.

4 Complete the mini-conversations with one word in each gap.

Imelda Personally, I ¹think that smartphones are a great invention.

Nick Yes, I ²a_____. I couldn't live without one.

Brendan That's probably ³t_____, Nick, but it doesn't mean you have to use yours all the time!

Sarah In my ⁴o_____, life is better now than when our parents were teenagers.

Tessa I'm ⁵n_____ sure about that. They didn't have social media, but they had a lot of hobbies.

Tracey You're ⁶r_____, Tessa. My dad says his teenage years were great fun.

Joel I'm ⁷s_____ that we'll have driverless cars soon.

Eli I think so ⁸t_____.

Ezra I'm ⁹s_____ but I don't agree. Not on the roads. They're too dangerous.

5 🔊 63 Put the sentences in order to make a conversation. Listen and check.

a ☐ 1 **Gina** What do you think about tablets?

b ☐ **Gina** What do you think, Sean?

c ☐ **Gina** Really? Why not? I think they're great. They're better than laptops.

d ☐ **Vicky** I'm sorry, but I don't agree. For films, games or school work, laptops are much better. For games and photos, I can use my phone.

e ☐ **Vicky** Well, in my opinion, I don't think they're very useful.

f ☐ **Sean** I agree with Vicky. I've got one but I don't often use it.

8F READING AND VOCABULARY

1 Read the text quickly and tick the things it mentions about technology.

Good

1 ☑ It's a source of information.
2 ☐ You can contact friends and relatives.
3 ☐ You never get lost.
4 ☐ You can get in touch with new people.
5 ☐ It helps people with special abilities to get noticed.
6 ☐ You never get bored.

Bad

7 ☐ It's a source of untrue information.
8 ☐ It's expensive.
9 ☐ It leaves less time for work and friends.
10 ☐ It makes you think other people have better lives.
11 ☐ It causes arguments with friends.

2 Read the text again. Match sentences A–G with gaps 1–5 in the text. There are two extra sentences.

A People are often amazed when they realise how many untrue articles there are online.

B One of these is the ability to hide our real personalities.

C People feel sad that their own lives don't seem so special.

D We can email them, text them or even make video phone calls.

E So how can governments control the social media companies?

F They can easily show their talents online and become famous.

G But does it make our lives better or worse?

Vocabulary extension

3 Match the highlighted words from the text with the definitions.

1 The right to enter a place or use a service such as a website. *access*
2 Join two things together. _____
3 To communicate with someone. _____
4 Friendships, family connections or romantic partnerships. _____
5 The information on a website. _____
6 Talk in a friendly way or exchange messages online.
_____

ACTIVE VOCABULARY | *Make + noun + (comparative) adjective*

In English, we often use the construction *make +* (comparative) adjective.

Music **makes me happy**.

The big windows **make the room brighter**.

4 Complete the second sentence using *make* and the words from the box. You might need to use the comparative form of the adjective.

it/big it/easy me/lazy our lives/good people/rich ~~teenagers/tired~~

1 Teenagers feel tired when they spend a lot of time playing video games.
Playing video games can *make teenagers tired*.

2 We can keep in touch with people more easily because of the Internet.
The Internet _____ to keep in touch with people.

3 Are we happier with social media?
Do social media _____?

4 I need to increase the size of the text on the screen because it's too small.
I can't read this text. I need to _____.

5 Talented people can earn a lot of money from online videos.
The Internet can _____.

6 I don't learn skills like map reading because my phone can do everything for me.
My mobile phone _____!

5 Complete the sentences with the phrases from Exercise 4.

1 Our garage is too small for our new car. We need to ask some builders to *make it bigger*.

2 A job in finance can _____ but it may also make them more stressed.

3 Do expensive gadgets _____ or not?

4 Staying up late can _____ at school the next day.

5 I like the summer but it _____. I don't want to do anything, I just want to lie in the sun!

6 This new app _____ to book cheap plane tickets! It's much better than the old one.

6 ON A HIGH NOTE Write about things you like about technology or social media and things you don't like about them.

modern technology –

is it a good thing or not?

The world today is a very different place to the world of forty years ago. Technology is very important in our lives: at work, at home, when travelling and meeting people. ¹___. Read on and find out.

Our lives are, in many ways, easier because of technology. We have access to more information than ever before. We can also keep in touch with family and friends easily. ²___ It is also possible to connect with other people around the world. Although we might never meet them in real life, we can chat with them and learn about their lives. In addition, technology gives creative people great opportunities. ³___ You only have to look at all the video stars and successful bloggers to see how we can use technology to show other people what we can do.

However, technology also has disadvantages. We hear a lot about fake news nowadays and it is very easy to use technology to make people believe false information, especially with photo and video editing tools. ⁴___ Gadgets and social media can also make us more tired at work and at school. They leave us less time for 'real' life and relationships.

In addition, surveys show that social media can be a major cause of depression, especially in young people. One reason for this is that most people only post exciting news and beautiful photos, so it can appear that all our friends have perfect lives. ⁵___ Even those who become successful through social media are not always as happy as they seem. Many become stressed because they need to produce new content all the time. They are scared that they will lose the viewers and subscribers they need to earn money.

So, is technology good or bad for us? My answer is that you can't avoid it so make the most of it but make sure you use it carefully and with self-control.

8G WRITING | A notice

MISSING/CAN YOU HELP?

What? A black ²_laptop bag_. Inside there are
three ²_____ with personal photos on them.
They are very important to me.

Where? Under the ³_____ next to the window in this café.

When? ⁴_____ , June 16th at about ⁵_____.

The laptop bag is old and not very important but,
please, help me to find my CDs.
I don't have any other copies of the photos on them.

REWARD: ⁶_____ !!

Contact Russell Stevens.
⁷_____ 439431323 **or email:** Russ.Stevens17@eemail.com

Write a big heading.

Use colours.

Add a simple description.

Write where and when you lost the item.

Add a photo of the item missing.

Offer a reward.

Give your name and contact details.

1 Complete the notice with the words from the box.

£20   5 p.m.   CDs   Friday   ~~laptop bag~~   table   text

2 Eden wants to sell a laptop. Look at the ideas below. Tick the things that she should include in the notice.
1 ☑ A heading saying: For sale
2 ☐ Silver
3 ☐ Cost £500 new
4 ☐ 500GB hard drive
5 ☐ I bought it in London
6 ☐ 14" laptop
7 ☐ Contact: Eden Sloane, Class 10B
8 ☐ Good condition
9 ☐ I use it to do homework on
10 ☐ Three years old
11 ☐ £100

3 Complete the notice about the laptop with the information you ticked in Exercise 2.

FOR SALE!
Silver 14" laptop
ONLY £100
_____
_____
_____

4 WRITING TASK Write two notices.
A You lost a video game on the school bus last Thursday. Describe the game and offer a reward.
B You want to sell a camera. Describe the camera and say how much you want for it.

ACTIVE WRITING | A notice
1 Plan your notices.
- Think of the information you want to include.
- Decide how to design your notices.

2 Write the notices.
- Use colours and different sized fonts to make the notices clear and eye-catching.
- Include important information.
- Don't include unnecessary information.
- Don't forget to include contact details at the end.

3 Check that ...
- you have included all the relevant information.
- there are no spelling or grammar mistakes.
- your notices are likely to attract attention.

96

UNIT VOCABULARY PRACTICE

1 8A GRAMMAR AND VOCABULARY **Match the gadgets from the box with the descriptions.**

charger ~~drone~~ headphones health tracker
smartphone tablet computer 3D printer
virtual reality headset

1 You can control this, make it fly and take photos or films with it. *drone*

2 You can design objects on your computer and then create them with this gadget. _____

3 This keeps your battery full. _____

4 A phone which has many functions of a computer. _____

5 You wear these and listen to music through them. _____

6 This keeps a record of how much exercise you do each day. _____

7 This looks a bit like a big mobile phone – but it isn't a phone. _____

8 When you wear this, you feel as if you are somewhere completely different. _____

2 8B VOCABULARY **Complete the text with the words from the box.**

app ~~battery~~ cables charge hard install
keyboard print save scan screen speakers type
webcam

Laptop for Sale £450

This is a great offer. The ¹*battery* lasts for seven hours before you need to ²_____ it. The ³_____ is big so it's great for watching films. The ⁴_____ disk has 1000GB of space on it.

The laptop comes with two small ⁵_____ for better sound, a wireless ⁶_____ with letters that light up in the dark – great if you want to ⁷_____ at night and don't want to switch on the bedroom light. You can connect four USB ⁸_____ to the laptop at one time.

We can ⁹_____ some great programs on the laptop to make your life even easier. You can choose a great anti-virus program or one of the best photo editing programs available.

The laptop has an excellent ¹⁰_____ for video calls (you will look and sound amazing!) and we're also offering a FREE 3-in-one printer. You can ¹¹_____ paper copies of documents, ¹²_____ photos and ¹³_____ them on the laptop as well as make photocopies.

Don't delay. This special offer finishes on Saturday.

For more offers, check out our website or download our free mobile phone ¹⁴_____.

3 8D LISTENING AND VOCABULARY **Choose the correct words to complete the sentences.**

1 You can't take people into space on holiday before you __ the spaceship and make sure it is safe.
   a discover   **b** test   **c** experiment

2 This company __ expensive smartwatches. They only make about 200 a year but they make a lot of money.
   a invents   **b** produces   **c** discovers

3 When I bought my camera, I enjoyed __ with different settings to see what the photos looked like.
   a testing   **b** developing   **c** experimenting

4 Last year, tech companies __ great apps for having video calls.
   a developed   **b** experimented   **c** discovered

5 Do you think that when we travel to different planets, we may __ a completely new colour?
   a test   **b** invent   **c** discover

4 8F READING AND VOCABULARY **Complete the sentences with adjectives. The adjectives begin with the same letter as the people's names.**

1 Annabelle was *amazed* that I remembered her. We were nine years old when she moved away.

2 William is _____ because he can't find his wallet.

3 Sonia is _____ because it's dark, and she is alone.

4 Arthur is _____ because his sister broke his smartphone.

5 Simon is _____ because it's his birthday, and no one remembered.

6 Sam is _____ because she's got an important exam tomorrow.

7 Harry is _____ that it's the weekend.

8 Sol was _____ when he got a letter from Turkey because he doesn't know anyone there.

9 Eve is _____ because she's flying to New York tomorrow. She loves visiting new places.

5 ON A HIGH NOTE **Write about times when you felt different emotions and explain why you felt like that.**

1 For each learning objective, write 1–5 to assess your ability.

1 = I don't feel confident. 5 = I feel confident.

	Learning objective	Course material	How confident I am (1–5)
8A	I can use *will/ won't* to make predictions about the future.	Student's Book pp. 102–103 Workbook pp. 88–89	
8B	I can talk about computers.	Student's Book p. 104 Workbook p. 90	
8C	I can use adverbs to talk about the way we do things.	Student's Book p. 105 Workbook p. 91	
8D	I can identify the main points in a conversation and talk about technology.	Student's Book p. 106 Workbook p. 92	
8E	I can express, agree and disagree with opinions.	Student's Book p. 107 Workbook p. 93	
8F	I can identify the structure of a text and talk about feelings and communication.	Student's Book pp. 108–109 Workbook pp. 94–95	
8G	I can write a short notice.	Student's Book p. 110 Workbook pp. 96	

2 Which of the skills above would you like to improve in? How?

Skill I want to improve in	How I can improve

3 What can you remember from this unit?

New words I learned and most want to remember	Expressions and phrases I liked	English I heard or read outside class

GRAMMAR AND VOCABULARY

1 Choose the correct words to complete the sentences.

1 I'm ___. I've got nothing to do.
   a bored **b** worried **c** stressed
2 We're going to ___ a very light but strong laptop in our factory.
   a experiment **b** develop **c** discover
3 I ___ the tickets. Here's yours. Don't lose it.
   a saved **b** printed **c** typed
4 You should get a health ___. It gives you lots of information about your exercise and diet.
   a scanner **b** charger **c** tracker
5 Hi, I got the email, but you forgot to ___ the photo! Can you send it?
   a attach **b** delete **c** install

/ 5

2 Complete the sentences with the words from the box.

delete   drone   headphones   ~~installed~~   produces   type

1 I *installed* new computer software. It's great for making professional looking websites.
2 Our teacher says we have to write our essay with a pen. We can't ___ it and print it.
3 Take off your ___. I tried to call you, but you couldn't hear me.
4 I'm going to ___ some of these files. I don't need them.
5 This computer games company ___ good games.
6 We can take some photos of our street with my new ___. It's easy to control where it flies.

/ 5

3 Use the prompts to write questions using *will*.

Hazel   It's great that you can come to my party on Friday, Eduardo. What time / arrive?
   ¹*What time will you arrive*?
Eduardo   About 7 p.m.
Hazel   able / find / the house?
   2 ___
Eduardo   Yes, I'm sure I will. Don't worry.
Hazel   How long / able / stay?
   3 ___
Eduardo   Until 10.30. That's when the last bus leaves. How many people / be / at the party?
   4 ___
Hazel   About 20.
Eduardo   know / them all?
   5 ___
Hazel   No, there will be some people you don't know. That isn't a problem, is it?
Eduardo   No, of course not. there / food / at the party?
   6 ___
Hazel   There will be pizza and snacks.
Eduardo   Great. See you on Friday.

/ 5

4 Complete reasons 1–6 with the correct forms of the words in brackets. Then match them with results a–f.

1 ☐ I write very *untidily* (untidy).
2 ☐ My computer works very ___ (slow).
3 ☐ My teacher speaks very ___ (quiet).
4 ☐ Beth runs really ___ (fast).
5 ☐ These students speak too ___ (quick).
6 ☐ I sang really ___ (bad).

a My teacher can't read my essay.
b She often wins school sports competitions.
c No one liked my performance in the school show.
d I need a new one.
e I can't understand them.
f I can't hear him.

/ 5

USE OF ENGLISH

5 Complete the sentences with the correct words formed from the words in bold.

1 Before you buy the phone, check it very *carefully* to make sure it's OK. **CAREFUL**
2 The most important things to take on holiday are a phone and a phone ___! **CHARGE**
3 I've got some ___ headphones. I don't need to connect them to my phone with a cable. **WIRE**
4 We played ___ but we didn't win the match. **GOOD**
5 This virtual ___ headset is amazing. **REAL**
6 My younger brothers were playing together ___ so I went downstairs to watch TV. **HAPPY**

/ 5

6 Complete the texts with one word in each gap.

Re: laptop

I rang the computer company and they **¹*will*** send the parts you need next week. With the new hard **2** ___, I will be **3** ___ to fix it quite easily.

Re: battery

There's a problem with your battery. I tried to **4** ___ it yesterday but after four hours it was only 50% full. When I tested it, it stopped working after just ten minutes. I think you need to buy a new battery.

Re: speaker

The reason your speaker doesn't work is that it isn't a wireless speaker! You need to connect it to your laptop with a USB **5** ___. Don't **6** ___ up the volume too much before you switch it on – it's very loud!

/ 5

/ 30

99

Fit and healthy

9A GRAMMAR AND VOCABULARY

Must/mustn't/have to/don't have to

1 ★ Look at the information and decide if the sentences are true or false.

> ## Walking Club
>
> Free club for students in Years 8–13. The club is for everyone – even those who aren't fit. If you are interested, take a copy of the letter home to your parents and ask them to sign it. Bring the letter to the first meeting of the club. You can't attend without your parents' signatures.
>
> No special equipment needed. Bring shorts, a T-shirt and trainers. The first walk is a 4.4 km walk from the school through the park. Stay with the group at all times.

1 ☐ You have to pay to join the club.
2 ☐ Students must be in Year 8 or above.
3 ☐ You must be fit.
4 ☐ Your parents must sign the letter.
5 ☐ You don't have to bring the letter to the first meeting.
6 ☐ You don't have to bring any special equipment.
7 ☐ You don't have to wear trainers.
8 ☐ You have to stay with the group when you walk.

2 ★ Choose the correct words to complete the sentences. Sometimes both options are possible.

1 You *mustn't / don't have to* wear swimming trunks. You can wear shorts if you prefer.
2 You *mustn't / don't have to* use your hands when playing football. You can only use your feet or head.
3 You *must / have to* have a ball to play basketball.
4 We *mustn't / don't have to* play football at our school. We can choose other sports.
5 You *must / have to* arrive early for the match.
6 Running is cheap because you *mustn't / don't have to* have any special equipment.
7 You *mustn't / don't have to* join a gym to get fit. You can go running or cycling.
8 Parents *mustn't / don't have to* take photos at sports day. It is not allowed.

3 ★★ Complete the text with the correct forms of the verbs in brackets. Use *have to/don't have to* or *must/ mustn't*. Sometimes both options are possible.

> Some people think horse riding is easy. You ¹*don't have to do* (not/do) anything. You just get on the horse and the horse ²_____ (do) all the work. Well, it isn't quite like that. Firstly, we ³_____ (get) all the equipment ready and put it on the horse.
>
> When you're a new rider, you ⁴_____ (always/ listen) carefully to what the instructor says and you ⁵_____ (not/go) too fast or do anything dangerous.
>
> At the end of the lesson, we ⁶_____ (take off) all the equipment and put it away. Then we ⁷_____ (clean) the horses and give them food. We ⁸_____ (not/leave) until we finish everything. Luckily, we ⁹_____ (not/look after) the horses on other days – someone else looks after them.

4 ★★ Look at the poster and complete the sentences with *have to*, *don't have to* or *mustn't*.

> ## TENNIS COMPETITION
>
> **Show your ticket at the gate.**
> **Sit in the correct seat.**
> **Don't walk on the grass.**
> **Be quiet during the game.**
> **You can arrive late and leave early BUT please try not to disturb other people.**
> **No food or drink** (you can get water here).

1 You *have to* show your ticket at the gate.
2 You _____ sit in the correct seat.
3 You _____ walk on the grass.
4 You _____ shout.
5 You _____ arrive on time.
6 You _____ stay until the end.
7 You _____ bring food or drink.

5 ★★ Complete the dialogue with the phrases from the box.

---

do you have to be   do you have to wear   don't have to be
~~have to be~~   have to run   have to throw
have to understand

Henry	See if you can guess the sport.
Lou	OK.
Henry	You **¹*have to be*** very strong.
Lou	Boxing?
Henry	No. OK, you can ask a question now.
Lou	**²**_____ special clothes?
Henry	Yes, you do. OK, next clue. You **³**_____ the rules.
Lou	That doesn't help much!
Henry	OK, you **⁴**_____ very fast and you **⁵**_____ the ball a long way.
Lou	Oh, OK. **⁶**_____ American to play?
Henry	No, you **⁷**_____ American but most people who play it are American.
Lou	I know. American football.
Henry	Very good. Your turn.

6 ★★★ USE OF ENGLISH Choose the correct words a–c to complete the text.

Cheese rolling is a very special and very dangerous sport. There is a hill in England where, every year, a big, round cheese rolls down the hill and people run after it. You **¹**___ have any special equipment but you **²**___ be very careful. You **³**___ run too fast because it's easy to fall. Every year some people **⁴**___ go to hospital, often with broken bones. To win the competition you **⁵**___ catch the cheese – that isn't possible. You just **⁶**___ to be the first person to get to the bottom of the hill. The cheese isn't actually important at all. It just gives people a reason to run down the hill as fast as they can!

1	**a** have to	**b** mustn't	**c** don't have to
2	**a** must	**b** don't have to	**c** have
3	**a** don't have to	**b** must	**c** mustn't
4	**a** mustn't	**b** have to	**c** don't have to
5	**a** have to	**b** must	**c** don't have to
6	**a** must	**b** have	**c** don't have

7 ★★★ Complete the second sentence with one word or contraction in each gap so that it means the same as the first one.

1 It's necessary to train every day.
You **_must train_** every day.

2 It isn't necessary for students to join this club.
Students _____ _____ _____ _____ this club.

3 Players are not allowed to argue with the manager's decisions.
Players _____ _____ with the manager's decisions.

4 It isn't necessary for you to buy any equipment.
You _____ _____ _____ _____ any equipment.

5 It's necessary for team members to wear the official team shorts and T-shirt.
Team members _____ _____ _____ the official team shorts and T-shirt.

6 Don't do anything dangerous when you're playing.
You _____ _____ anything dangerous when you're playing.

8 ON A HIGH NOTE Write about some things you have to do, don't have to do or mustn't do at home and at school.

9B LISTENING AND VOCABULARY

1 🔊 **64 Listen and match conversations 1–3 with activities a–c.**

1 ☐   **a** mountain biking
2 ☐   **b** walking
3 ☐   **c** swimming

2 🔊 **64 Listen to the conversations again and choose the correct answers.**

1 Which clothes did the speaker not wear?

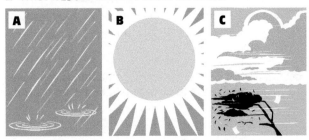

2 What was the weather like in Cornwall?

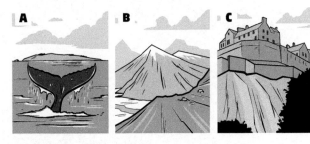

3 What did the boy see while mountain biking?

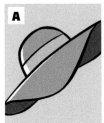

Vocabulary extension

3 🔊 **65 Complete the extracts from the recording in Exercise 1 with positive adjectives. Listen and check.**

1 'How was your holiday?'
'A*mazin*g! We went on a 19 km walk in the mountains.'
2 'So did your brother go surfing?'
'Yes. He had a b_____t time.'
3 'How was Scotland?'
'W_____l! We were there for two weeks.'
4 And the views from the top of the hills were a_____e!'
5 On another day, we went to an island on a ferry and saw some whales. That was g_____t.

4 **ON A HIGH NOTE Describe an activity you can do somewhere in your country. Explain why it is a good place to do the activity.**

Pronunciation

> ### ACTIVE PRONUNCIATION | Intonation to show emotion
>
> We use intonation to show emotion when telling a story or responding to what someone says. The stressed syllable is even more stressed than usual:
> *That's fanTAStic!*
> We can also use intonation to show surprise in a question.
> *'I won a dance competition last week.' 'A **DANCE** competition?'*

5 🔊 **66 Listen to two different people saying the same sentences. Who shows their feelings more in each sentence? Choose a or b?**

1 'How was your holiday?' 'Amazing!'   a / b
2 Luckily, it didn't rain but it was still really cold on the beach.   a / b
3 I wasn't worried about the danger, but the water was freezing!   a / b
4 It was beautiful!   a / b
5 We came down really fast!   a / b
6 That was great!   a / b

6 🔊 **67 Listen to the sentences again and repeat them to show your feelings.**

7 🔊 **68 We can also use intonation to show surprise. This can turn a one-word response into a question. Listen to an extract from the recording in Exercise 1 and repeat the response with the correct intonation.**

Josie   I went to Cornwall in the west of England last year. My brother wanted to go surfing.
Martin   Surfing? In England?

8 🔊 **69 Say the responses and show your surprise using the correct intonation. Then listen to the recording and copy the intonation of the speakers.**

Amy   I got 100% in my English test.
Suzie   Really? In English?

Jack   I want to be a famous sports star.
Alice   A sports star? But you wanted to be a photographer only a few days ago!

Chuck   My dad's 50 this weekend.
Brad   Fifty? Your dad?

Miley   I got an email from Alice last night.
Trace   An email? From Alice?

Peter   We swam in the sea on Saturday.
Sam   You swam? In the sea? In April?

9C **VOCABULARY** | Body

1 ⭐ Complete the crossword with the words you can see in the picture.

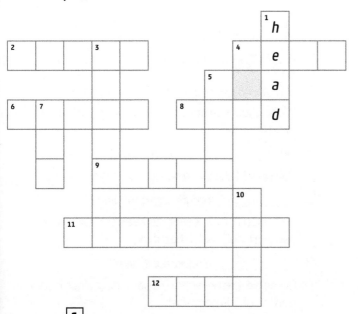

Crossword grid with:
- 1 down: h e a d

2 ⭐ Match the words from the box with the definitions.

ears   eyes   fingers   ~~knee~~   mouth   nose   toes

1 This is a part of the leg. It helps you to bend the leg. _knee_

2 You have five of these on each foot. _____

3 You use this to smell things. _____

4 You use this to eat and talk. _____

5 You have five of these on each hand. _____

6 You use these to see things with. _____

7 You need these when you listen to music. _____

3 ⭐ Complete the sentences with the names of the people in the picture.

1 _____ is thin.   **3** _____ is strong.

2 _____ is slim.   **4** _____ is weak.

Hermann

Percy

Meghan

4 ⭐⭐ Look at the picture in Exercise 3 and complete the descriptions with the words from the box.

elbows   flat   narrow   round   ~~stomach~~   weak   wide

Hermann goes to the gym every day. He has big muscles. His arms, legs and ¹_stomach_ are like a rock. He has very ²_____ shoulders. It's difficult for him to find shirts that fit him.

It's Percy's first day at the gym. He can't lift any weights. He has very ³_____ arms with no muscles in them at all. His ⁴_____ are just skin and bone!

Meghan is very fit. She has ⁵_____ shoulders and a ⁶_____ stomach. In the past she didn't care about the right food and exercise so her stomach was ⁷_____ like a ball.

5 ON A HIGH NOTE Describe yourself e.g. *I've got brown eyes/long legs*, etc. Describe your friends or people in your family as well.

Should/shouldn't

1 ⭐ Complete the sentences with *should* and the verbs in brackets.

1 You *shouldn't try* (not try) to do too much exercise.

2 You _____ (not laugh) at people who aren't very good at sport.

3 We _____ (help) the new players become even better.

4 _____ (I/get) a health tracker?

5 You _____ (not do) exercise after a big meal.

6 Which sport _____ (I/choose?)

7 You _____ (always/warm up) before you play sports.

8 _____ (we/wear) gloves when we play?

2 ⭐⭐ Put the words in order to complete the dialogue.

Jan Oh, no. We've got PE later. I haven't got my trainers.

Rita in the evening / in / should / them / bag / put / your / you

1 *You should put them in your bag in the evening.*

Jan I know, I always forget in the morning. I never have any time.

tell / what / I / Mr Lewis / should / ?

2 _____

Rita tell / the / should / truth / him / you

3 _____

Jan and / go / get / I / home / them / should / ?

4 _____

Rita No, you can't. We've got Maths now. You can't miss Maths. That's worse than missing PE.

Rita Mr Lewis / see / now / should / to / you / go

5 _____

He can think of something for you to do during the lesson.

Jan Like what?

Rita I don't know. Maybe write 100 times, 'not / should / trainers / forget / I / my'

6 _____

Jan Oh, great! Thanks! I'm glad you aren't my teacher.

3 ⭐⭐ Read the answers and complete the questions.

FAQ for people thinking of entering the Marathon next June

1 *How much exercise should I do* **every day?**
We suggest you start by doing about one hour of exercise a day.

2 *When* _____ **for the race?**
You should start training as soon as you can.

3 _____ **before I start training?**
It shouldn't be necessary to see a doctor before you start, but it isn't a bad thing.

4 _____ **a personal trainer?**
Some people like to have a personal trainer, but we don't think it is necessary.

5 *What* _____ **before the race?**
Don't eat a big meal before the race but, about an hour before the start it is good to eat something like a yoghurt with honey, a banana and some nuts or other snacks to give you energy.

6 *What* _____ **during the race?**
You should wear a T-shirt, shorts and comfortable, good quality running shoes.

7 _____ **with a friend?**
For your first marathon it's a great idea to run with a friend. You can help each other.

8 *What* _____ **when the race finishes?**
When the race finishes, you should put on something warm – the organisers will give you a special blanket. Try to eat something – another banana for example – and, when you get home, try an ice-cold bath!

4 ⭐⭐⭐ Complete the sentences with *should* or *shouldn't* and the correct verbs.

1 My brother is unfit. He *should do* more exercise. He *shouldn't play* computer games every day.

2 My sister doesn't have much time. She _____ so much time on her phone.

3 My dad is always tired. He _____ to bed earlier.

4 My mother wants to be healthier. She _____ more vegetables and less fast food.

5 I want to get fit. I _____ so lazy!

6 We all need to go on more walks. We _____ our neighbour's dog for walks in the park.

5 ON A HIGH NOTE Think of a hobby or activity you do. Give someone advice about what your friend should or shouldn't do if he/she wants to do the same activity.

9E SPEAKING

1 🔊 *70* Listen and repeat the phrases. How do you say them in your language?

SPEAKING | Talking about illness

ASKING ABOUT SOMEONE'S HEALTH

What's the matter?

How are you feeling?

Are you feeling alright?

What's wrong?

DESCRIBING HOW YOU'RE FEELING/SYMPTOMS

I don't feel well.

I feel sick.

I can't sleep.

I've got a sore throat.

My stomach hurts.

I feel (a lot) better.

SHOWING SYMPATHY

I hope you feel better soon.

Get well soon.

GIVING ADVICE

You should try to eat some breakfast.

You shouldn't go to school today.

You must go to bed.

Why don't you go to see the doctor?

---

2 Complete the sentences with one word in each gap.

1 I've got a sore *throat*.
2 What's the m_____?
3 Get well s_____.
4 How are you f_____?
5 I don't feel w_____.
6 What's w_____?
7 I feel much b_____ today.
8 My knee h_____.
9 I can't s_____ at night so I'm always tired during the day.

3 Match sentences 1–6 with responses a–f.

1 ☐ What's the matter?
2 ☐ How are you feeling today?
3 ☐ Get well soon.
4 ☐ I've got toothache.
5 ☐ I feel sick.
6 ☐ I've got a headache.

a Well, don't eat that burger.
b Much better, thanks.
c You should go to the dentist.
d Nothing serious. My back hurts a bit.
e You should take an aspirin and lie down.
f Thank you.

4 Complete the mini-conversations with the phrases from the box.

A lot better, thanks   But it's boring in bed   I can't move
I feel sick   ~~No, not really~~   Oh, no. I can't   OK, thanks
OK, where's my phone

Greg Are you feeling alright?
Simon ¹*No, not really*. My back hurts.
Greg Why don't you lie down?
Simon OK, but can you help me into bed, please?
² _____.

Alice How are you feeling?
Lucy ³ _____ but I've got a sore throat.
Alice You should drink this tea with honey and lemon.
Lucy ⁴ _____. Mmm, it's delicious.

Mark You should eat some breakfast.
Paula ⁵ _____.
Mark Why not? What's the matter?
Paula ⁶ _____.

Noah You must go to bed. That's what the doctor said.
Sarah ⁷ _____.
Noah Why don't you read?
Sarah ⁸ _____?
Noah Not your phone. A book!

5 🔊 *71* Complete the dialogue with one word in each gap. Listen and check.

Doctor Good morning. What's ¹*wrong*?
Patient I feel sick, my stomach ² _____ and I've got a ³ _____ throat.
Doctor Oh, dear. Let me take a look. Mmm. Well, it's nothing too serious but you ⁴ _____ go to bed. Come back and see me in a week.

A week later ...

Doctor Ah, hello. How are you ⁵ _____ ?
Patient A ⁶ _____ better, thank you.
Doctor Good, good. Let's have a look. Yes, everything seems fine ... Ooooh!
Patient What's the ⁷ _____, doctor?
Doctor I don't feel ⁸ _____.
Patient ⁹ _____ don't you go home? There aren't any more patients. I'm the last one.
Doctor Good idea.

9F READING AND VOCABULARY

1 Read the text quickly and match headings A–E with paragraphs 1–5.

   A Is it safe?

   B What does the qualification allow me to do?

   C What equipment do I need?

   D What does the course involve?

   E Is it difficult?

2 Read the text again and choose the correct answers.

   1 People taking the course

     a spend all their time underwater.

     b sometimes have to dive without instructors.

     c have to do two kinds of tests at the end.

     d learn how to save themselves in dangerous situations.

   2 According to the text

     a you should pass the course because you get a lot of help.

     b everyone should easily pass the test.

     c you need to have swimming qualifications to take the course.

     d you don't need to work hard to pass the test.

   3 Which of these facts is correct?

     a All students must get a medical certificate before they start the course.

     b The first thing the students do is to practise diving in a swimming pool.

     c The first dive in the sea doesn't take place on the first three days of the course.

     d Each student has their own, personal instructor.

   4 Which of these does NOT describe the equipment the company provides?

     a It is new.

     b They look after it well.

     c There is a big variety.

     d It's made for students.

   5 After taking the course, students

     a can only dive with organised groups.

     b can't dive until they take another test.

     c can only dive in certain parts of the world.

     d are only qualified for some kinds of diving.

   6 Which of these sentences would best fit the introduction (gap A)?

     a Now that you are on the course, here are some facts you need to know to help you pass.

     b Before you decide to take one of our courses, please read this text carefully and contact us if you have any other questions.

     c Find out why diving is the perfect way to spend your free time.

     d Read on to find out why we are the world's best diving school.

Vocabulary extension

3 Match the highlighted words from the text with the definitions.

   1 The things you need to do an activity. _equipment_

   2 People who are learning something for the first time and don't know anything about it. _____

   3 A high level. _____

   4 Pieces of work that somebody has to do. _____

   5 An official piece of paper which says you have passed and exam or course. _____

   6 People who teach a sport or a practical skill. _____

4 Complete the sentences with the correct forms of the words from Exercise 3.

   1 We have an _advanced_ course for people who can already ski well.

   2 In history class, we worked on a project and had to complete a few _____ in groups.

   3 I'd like to learn Italian but I'm a complete _____. I don't even know how to say 'Hello'.

   4 The only _____ you need for the photography course is a camera.

   5 I keep all my _____ from school in a folder so I don't lose them.

   6 Sheila is a driving _____. She teaches people how to drive.

ACTIVE VOCABULARY | Suffix *-ous*

In English, many adjectives end in *-ous* (e.g. ser**ious**).

---

5 Complete the sentences with the words from the box.

---

dangerous enormous famous nervous obvious ~~serious~~ various

---

   1 The trainers were friendly but very _serious_. They didn't laugh and joke during the lessons.

   2 Everyone is taking that woman's photo. Do you think she's _____?

   3 We were under the water when I saw an _____ fish. Honestly, it was about three metres long.

   4 Let's climb this mountain. Don't worry, it isn't _____. Even children can do it safely.

   5 I think it's quite _____ that you won't be able to speak Swedish perfectly after a one-year course.

   6 How are you feeling? _____? Don't worry. You'll pass the test easily.

   7 There are _____ activities that you can do.

6 ON A HIGH NOTE Find out about a course you would like to take and write a short paragraph about what you have to do to pass it and what you can do after that.

UNDERWATER ADVENTURE

We are the biggest diving course training school in the world with over 30 centres and 2000 successful new divers a year. A_

1 ☐ You will learn how to dive safely, you will be able to use the equipment we give you and you will know what to do in different, surprising situations with our instructors watching you carefully at all times. There are various tasks that you have to complete successfully. In one, you have to show that you can save someone who is having problems underwater. There are some classroom lessons about how diving affects the blood, heart and lungs, but most of the course we spend in the water. At the end of the course there are practical and written tests that you must pass.

2 ☐ The course is fairly easy but there is a lot of new information that you must learn, and the equipment is quite complicated. However, our instructors are all very professional and patient and are here to help you pass the tests. The only people who are unlikely to pass are those who think they can learn to dive without listening to instructions. We don't ask you for swimming certificates as you don't need to be a great swimmer to take the course, but it is important that you don't feel nervous in deep water.

3 ☐ Yes, totally. After some classroom training, we start by diving in swimming pools. You won't dive in the open ocean until we are sure you are ready, usually on the fourth or fifth day. So, by the time you dive in dangerous water, you will know exactly what you have to do to stay safe. And, of course, we have very small groups so that instructors can watch everyone closely. For people who have medical problems, we need a doctor's certificate to say that it is safe for you to take the course.

4 ☐ You don't need any. We have a wide range of all the latest, modern equipment which we keep in perfect condition. We use the same equipment as experienced divers as it is much better than equipment specially made for beginners.

5 ☐ This is a beginner's course. Once you pass this, you can go diving all over the world in water up to 18 metres deep. You can't dive alone. You have to dive with another person who has also got a diving certificate. We always recommend diving in larger groups until you have more experience. For more difficult diving, you need to take an advanced test.

9G **WRITING** | An online forum post

Advice column

Adrian (16)

My problem is that I'm not very good at team sports. I like sports. I play tennis and I **¹***also* go swimming every Saturday. I do a lot of cycling **²**_____.
In PE, though, we only have a choice of football or rugby and I feel bad about it. A lot of students are very serious about these sports. They play for the school team and some of them play for local teams **³**_____. They want to win and always choose me last.

I know I should do PE because exercise is good for me, but I really hate the lessons. Sometimes I tell the teacher that I feel sick and I **⁴**_____ often 'forget' to bring my trainers.

Please give me some advice on how I can enjoy PE lessons like the other students do.

Give details about the problem.

Say how you feel about it.

Explain why.

List the solutions tried.

Ask for advice.

1 Read the post and complete it with *too* or *also*.

2 Complete the sentences with *too* or *also*.

  1 I do a lot of cycling. My friend goes cycling *too*.
  2 I have a stomach ache. I _____ have a headache.
  3 We gave a presentation on healthy food and we _____ showed a short film about exercise.
  4 In the summer, we sometimes have lessons outside. We often go on school trips _____.
  5 I drink a lot of water. My parents drink a lot of water _____.
  6 At our school, there's a football pitch and a running track and there's _____ a great gym.

3 Complete sentences a–f with *too* or *also* and match them with sentences 1–6.

  1 ☐ In the summer, we often go swimming.
  2 ☐ You need a new bat.
  3 ☐ Jack speaks French really well.
  4 ☐ We ran 10 km.
  5 ☐ I overslept so I didn't have time for breakfast.
  6 ☐ What's wrong? You look tired.

  a We *also* had a 2 km swim.
  b You _____ look sad.
  c You need some new gloves _____.
  d I was late for training _____.
  e We _____ play tennis.
  f He _____ speaks Spanish and Italian.

4 WRITING TASK Write a post about one of the problems below.

  A You want to be a vegetarian, but you aren't very good at cooking and haven't got many ideas for tasty meals.

  B You did a lot of exercise when you were young, but you haven't got any free time for doing exercise now because of homework.

ACTIVE WRITING | An online forum post

1 Plan your post.
  • Choose the topic you want to write about.
  • Think of the information you want to include.

2 Write the post.
  • Start by explaining the problem.
  • Say how it makes you feel.
  • Explain why you feel the way you do.
  • Give details of the solutions you have tried.
  • Ask for advice.

3 Check that …
  • you have included all the relevant information.
  • there are no spelling or grammar mistakes.

UNIT VOCABULARY PRACTICE

1 9A GRAMMAR AND VOCABULARY **Choose the words which go with the verbs in bold. Sometimes more than one word is possible.**

1 **DO**   aerobics / basketball / judo
2 **GO**   climbing / hockey / karate
3 **GO**   rugby / horse riding / cycling
4 **DO**   yoga / athletics / swimming
5 **PLAY** skateboarding / tennis / volleyball
6 **GO**   football / gymnastics / kayaking

2 9B LISTENING AND VOCABULARY **Complete the sentences with the words from the box.**

bat goal goggles helmets ~~net~~ rackets trophy

1 In volleyball, you have to hit the ball over the _net_ with your hands.
2 We aren't in this competition to win a _____. We're here to have fun.
3 It's easy to hit the ball with a cricket _____ because it's quite big.
4 Let's play tennis. Here are some balls and I've got two _____ we can use.
5 Football is an easy game. You just need to get the ball in the other team's _____.
6 Cricketers started wearing _____ because some players got hit on the head by the ball.
7 I always wear _____ when I go swimming because my eyes get quite sore.

3 9C VOCABULARY **Complete the texts with one word in each gap.**

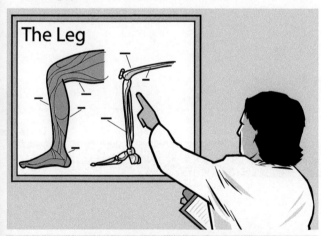

The Leg

Let's look at a human ¹_leg_. In the middle, we have a ²k_____. This helps us to walk and run. At the bottom of the leg is an ³a_____. This is a place where two bones come together. There are also muscles which should be ⁴s_____ if you want to run fast. We then have a ⁵f_____. As you can see, this one is quite ⁶w_____.

Let's look at this man's ⁷f_____. On his ⁸h_____ he is wearing a hat and he has a scarf around his ⁹n_____ to keep him warm. He's wearing glasses on his ¹⁰e_____. He needs them to read. We can't see the man's ¹¹e_____ because they are under his hat. It must be very cold because his ¹²n_____ is red. The man's ¹³m_____ is open and we can see his beautiful, white ¹⁴t_____.

4 9D GRAMMAR AND VOCABULARY **Match the two parts of the sentences.**

1 ☐ You should take   **a** ache.
2 ☐ I've got a sore   **b** sick.
3 ☐ I feel   **c** wrist hurts.
4 ☐ I've got a stomach   **d** temperature – 38,5°.
5 ☐ My ankle   **e** some aspirin.
6 ☐ I've got a high   **f** got a headache.
7 ☐ My   **g** throat.
8 ☐ I've   **h** hurts.

5 9F READING AND VOCABULARY **Choose the correct words to complete the sentences.**

1 Crossword puzzles, reading and learning languages help to keep your __ healthy and strong.
   a mind   **b** back   **c** muscle
2 I've got very white __ but when I lie in the sun, it turns a lovely brown colour.
   a blood   **b** skin   **c** heart
3 What is your most important __? The heart, I guess.
   a organ   **b** bone   **c** part
4 You need to do more exercise so that your __ get stronger.
   a organs   **b** blood   **c** muscles
5 Be careful when you go skiing. Don't fall over and break a __!
   a mouth   **b** muscle   **c** bone
6 Put your hand here. Can you feel your __ beating?
   a heart   **b** stomach   **c** blood
7 I cut my finger in the kitchen and now there's __ all over the table.
   a hair   **b** blood   **c** skin

6 ON A HIGH NOTE **We often talk about doing exercise to keep our bodies healthy. Write what you do to exercise your mind and keep it healthy.**

1 **For each learning objective, write 1–5 to assess your ability.**

1 = I don't feel confident. 5 = I feel confident.

	Learning objective	Course material	How confident I am (1–5)
9A	I can use *must, mustn't, have to, don't have to* to talk about necessity.	Student's Book pp. 116–117 Workbook pp. 100–101	
9B	I can identify specific information in a conversation and talk about sport.	Student's Book p. 118 Workbook p. 102	
9C	I can talk about body.	Student's Book p. 119 Workbook p. 103	
9D	I can use *should* and *shouldn't* to give an opinion or advice.	Student's Book p. 120 Workbook p. 104	
9E	I can ask about and talk about health and illness.	Student's Book p. 121 Workbook p. 105	
9F	I can identify specific information in a text and talk about health and fitness in space.	Student's Book pp. 122–123 Workbook pp. 106–107	
9G	I can write an online forum post.	Student's Book p. 124 Workbook p. 108	

2 **Which of the skills above would you like to improve in? How?**

Skill I want to improve in	How I can improve

3 **What can you remember from this unit?**

New words I learned and most want to remember	Expressions and phrases I liked	English I heard or read outside class

GRAMMAR AND VOCABULARY

1 Complete the sentences with the words from the box.

ache ~~goal~~ goggles karate mouth racket

1 When the other team get the ball, I want you all to run back and defend the _goal_.
2 You always get red eyes when you swim so wear some swimming _____.
3 After school, some students go to the gym and do _____.
4 Hit the ball with the _____.
5 Mum! I can't go to school today. I've got a stomach _____.
6 He liked the game so much that he watched it with his _____ wide open.

/ 5

2 Complete the text with the words from the box.

ankle bones ~~climbing~~ helmets hurt muscles

I went **¹**_climbing_ last weekend and now I'm in bed! The day started well. We all wore **²**_____ and I felt very safe. When we got back down, I decided to take a selfie on a rock. I fell when I took the photo! When I tried to stand, there was something wrong with my right **³**_____. It really **⁴**_____. Luckily, I didn't break any **⁵**_____ but I can't walk. When I feel better, I'm going to go swimming and cycling so my **⁶**_____ get strong again

/ 5

3 Use *should*, *must* and *mustn't* and the information below to complete the sentences.

Notes about the park. Some ideas for the local tourist information website.

PARK

Not allowed:	Good advice:	It's a rule:
• No cycling	• Go early when it's quiet.	• Leave before 8 p.m.
• No swimming in the lake	• Have lunch in the café.	• Walk on the paths.

Your advice for visitors
Places to visit > Park

Hi,
Anyone thinking of going to the park? Here are some things to think about.

1 You _should have_ lunch in the café. The food is delicious.
2 You _____ in the park. Leave your bike outside.
3 You _____ before 8 p.m.
4 You _____ in the lake!
5 You _____ on the paths – not on the grass.
6 You _____ early when the park is quiet.

Enjoy it!
Jane, 27 posts

/ 5

4 Complete the dialogue with *should, must, have to, shouldn't, mustn't* and *don't*. Use each word once.

Val   Ow. My tooth hurts.
Kyle   You **¹**_should_ go to the dentist.
Val   I hate going to the dentist. Do I **²**_____ go?
Kyle   No, you **³**_____ have to but I think it's a good idea.
Val   OK. I'll ask my parents to phone the dentist. But first, I want some chocolate.
Kyle   You **⁴**_____ eat chocolate.
Val   But I like chocolate.
Kyle   I know, but it's bad for your teeth.
Next day ...
Dentist   OK, it's ready. You **⁵**_____ eat anything for two hours. And you **⁶**_____ remember to brush your teeth twice a day.

/ 5

USE OF ENGLISH

5 Complete the second sentence using the word in bold so that it means the same as the first one. Use no more than three words including the word in bold.

1 You are not allowed to play football here. **MUST**
You _mustn't play_ football here.
2 My stomach hurts today. **ACHE**
I've got _____ today.
3 My advice for you is to go to bed. **SHOULD**
I think you _____ bed.
4 You need something to protect your eyes when you go swimming. **WEAR**
You should _____ when you go swimming.
5 You aren't very ill. You can go to school if you want or you can stay at home today. **HAVE**
You aren't very ill but you _____ to go to school today if you don't want to.
6 You're very quiet today. What's wrong? **MATTER**
You're very quiet today. What's _____?

/ 5

6 Choose the correct words a–c to complete the text.

It was my first horse riding lesson. Unfortunately, I fell off after five minutes. I didn't want to land on my head so I put my hands out and broke my **¹**__. Now I'm better but I don't want to go horse riding again – I want to find a new hobby. Mum says I **²**__ to choose something safe. I tried tennis but I couldn't get the ball over the **³**__! So today I'm **⁴**__ cycling with my friends. I know we should be careful and that we **⁵**__ cycle on busy roads, so I've got a map of cycle paths on my phone and we're going to follow them. I think it's going to be a great day.

1 a wrist	**b** muscle	**c** throat
2 a must	**b** should	**c** have
3 a trophy	**b** field	**c** net
4 a doing	**b** going	**c** playing
5 a shouldn't	**b** don't have to	**c** must

/ 5

/ 30

Our planet, our hands

10A GRAMMAR AND VOCABULARY

Present Perfect with *ever* and *never*

1 ★ Choose the correct words to complete the sentences.

1 I *have / has* been to Russia.

2 My mum *have / has* started a new job.

3 My grandparents haven't *flew / flown* in a plane.

4 Mr Davies *have / has* taught in South America.

5 My sister and I have *rode / ridden* on an elephant.

6 The students have *ever / never* organised a volunteer project.

7 You haven't *drove / driven* a car.

8 Has your dad *ever / never* slept in the desert?

2 ★ Rewrite the sentences with *ever* or *never* in the correct place.

1 Have you sung in a concert?

Have you ever sung in a concert?

2 Has your dad lived abroad?

_____

3 I've swum under a waterfall.

_____

4 My grandparents have used Facebook.

_____

5 Has your teacher forgotten his books?

_____

6 My mum's done judo.

_____

3 ★ Read the questions and write short answers.

1 Have you ever been to Venice?

✓ *Yes, I have.*

2 Has Mike seen your photos from Morocco?

✗ _____

3 Have your parents ever worked together?

✗ _____

4 Has Emma ever slept in a tent?

✓ _____

5 Have your friends ever organised a party together?

✓ _____

6 Have I ever scared you?

✗ _____

7 Has your local cinema ever shown any old black and white films?

✗ _____

4 ★ Complete the text with the correct Present Perfect forms of the verbs in brackets.

Hi! My name's Amy and my parents work for an international company. They never work in a country for more than two years. So, I'm now 15 and I ¹*have lived* (live) in eight different countries. I can't remember the first three countries but let me tell you about some of the things I ²_____ (do) in my life.

I ³_____ (swim) in the Indian Ocean.

I ⁴_____ (walk) in the Himalayas.

I ⁵_____ (eat) snakes.

I ⁶_____ (ride) on an elephant and a camel.

I ⁷_____ (met) teenagers from all over the world.

I ⁸_____ (take) photos of tigers in a jungle.

5 ★ Use the prompts to write questions in the Present Perfect.

1 How many times / you / fly / in a plane?
How many times have you flown in a plane?
2 How many countries / you / live in?
_____
3 Lisa / ever / do / any voluntary work?
_____
4 you and your sister / ever / be / on holiday without your parents?
_____
5 How many times / you / be / late for school this year?
_____
6 your parents / ever / ride / a motorbike?
_____
7 you / ever / meet / somebody famous?
_____
8 your friend / ever / lose / his phone?
_____

6 ★★ Put the words in order to make sentences.

1 never / friend / been / from / Brazil / my / the Amazon Jungle / has / to
My friend from Brazil has never been to the Amazon Jungle.
2 this / never / on / have / island / people / lived
_____
3 mountain / a teenager / this / has / climbed / ever / ?
_____
4 ever / desert / people / this / crossed / have / ?
_____
5 the ocean / children / seen / have / never / these
_____
6 beach / seen / this / you / of / a photo / ever / have / ?
_____
7 this / have / lake / in / swum / I / never
_____
8 red / ever / he / eaten / bananas / has / ?
_____

7 ★★ Complete the questions with the correct Present Perfect forms of the verbs from the box.

she/do ~~your dad/live~~ you/fly you/not read
you/spend you/take your grandmother/make
your mum/visit

1 How many countries *has your dad lived* in?
2 _____ in a helicopter?
3 Why _____ the book I gave you?
4 What interesting things _____ this year?
5 What kind of birthday cake _____ for you?
6 How much money _____ today?
7 How many exams _____ this week?
8 Which countries _____ this summer?

8 ★★★ Use the prompts to complete the mini-conversations in the Present Perfect.

Marcus you / ever / be / USA?
¹*Have you ever been to the USA?*
Jesse No / not. never / be / to America
² _____
Adrian you / hear / the news?
³ _____
Harry What news? I / not hear / any news
⁴ _____
Adrian The school / find / a new French teacher Everyone says she's great.
⁵ _____
Amir your / parents / ever / be / to China?
⁶ _____
Jake Yes / they. They / also be / to Japan but they / never / be / to India
⁷ _____

9 ★★★ USE OF ENGLISH Complete the text with one word in each gap.

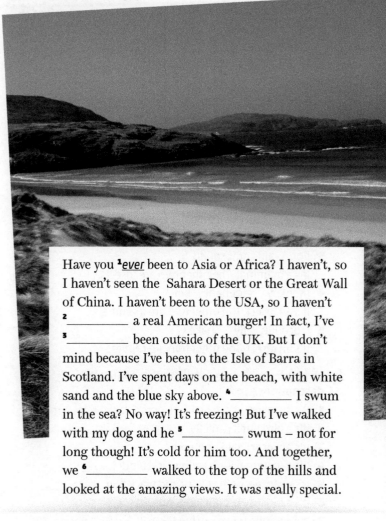

Have you ¹*ever* been to Asia or Africa? I haven't, so I haven't seen the Sahara Desert or the Great Wall of China. I haven't been to the USA, so I haven't ² _____ a real American burger! In fact, I've ³ _____ been outside of the UK. But I don't mind because I've been to the Isle of Barra in Scotland. I've spent days on the beach, with white sand and the blue sky above. ⁴ _____ I swum in the sea? No way! It's freezing! But I've walked with my dog and he ⁵ _____ swum – not for long though! It's cold for him too. And together, we ⁶ _____ walked to the top of the hills and looked at the amazing views. It was really special.

10 ON A HIGH NOTE Write about some interesting things you have done in your life and some things that you have never done but would like to do.

1 ⭐ Complete the crossword with the names of the animals in photos 1–10.

Crossword grid:

1 C
2 R
O
3 | 4 C
5 | 6 O
D
8 I
7 L
9 | 10 E

2 ⭐⭐ Find the odd one out in each group. Use the clues to help you.

1 penguin (dolphin) duck
It hasn't got wings. The other two have.

2 shark salmon whale
It's a mammal. The other two are fish.

3 lion ant mosquito
It's a mammal. The other two are insects.

4 monkey elephant bee
It's an insect. The other two are mammals.

5 crocodile fly snake
It's an insect. The other two are reptiles.

3 ⭐⭐ Write the names of animals to match the descriptions.

1 It's an insect. It can be black or red. It can bite! _ant_

2 It's a bird but it can't fly. _____

3 It's an insect. It likes blood. _____

4 It's a mammal with yellow and black fur. _____

5 It's an insect with yellow and black hair. _____

6 It's a big fish. It's got big teeth. _____

7 It's a reptile with very big teeth. It usually lives near lakes or rivers. _____

8 It lives in the ocean. It's friendly and intelligent. _____

4 ⭐⭐ Decide if the sentences are true or false.

1 ☐ A salmon has a beak.

2 ☐ A duck has feathers.

3 ☐ A penguin has a beak.

4 ☐ A shark has grey skin.

5 ☐ A mosquito has fur.

6 ☐ A dolphin has wings.

7 ☐ A whale has feathers.

8 ☐ A snake has teeth.

5 ON A HIGH NOTE Describe three different animals.

10C GRAMMAR

10

Present Perfect with *already, just* and *yet*

1 ★ Rewrite the sentences with the words in brackets in the correct place.

1 I haven't checked my phone. (yet)
I *haven't checked my phone yet.*

2 Our friends have got back from their holidays. (just)
_____

3 Have you bought a new bike? (yet)
_____

4 We've been here for six days. (already)
_____

5 I haven't seen any monkeys. (yet)
_____

6 I've finished the project on saving electricity. (already)
_____

7 We've watched a film about the environment. (just)
_____

8 Have you talked to your parents about the party? (yet)
_____

2 ★ Choose the correct words to complete the sentences.

1 Mum's *just / yet* gone to the shops. She won't be long.

2 Have you decided what to wear to the party *yet / already*?

3 We've been here for three days and we've *just / already* seen lots of things.

4 'Do your homework!' 'I've *already / yet* done it.'

5 We've been in the desert for a week and we haven't ridden on a camel *just / yet*.

6 Hello. You've arrived at the right time. I've *already / just* made some tea. Do you want some?

3 ★★ Complete the mini-conversations with *been* or *gone*.

Tessa Oh, look at all this food!
Ali Great! Mum's ¹*been* to the shops.

Nicky Where's Oliver? He isn't in his room.
Jason He's ² _____ out but I don't know where.

Dad So, are we going to the mountains this year?
Lucy I don't want to go there again. We've ³ _____ there lots of times.

Tom Where's the recycling bin? It was here and now it's ⁴ _____.
Andy It's around the corner. They moved it yesterday.

Mia When is Andrea going to China?
Paula She's already ⁵ _____. She left this morning.

Mollie Hi, Mum. Where have you ⁶ _____?
Mum I've ⁷ _____ to the gym. It was great.

4 ★★ USE OF ENGLISH Choose the correct words a–c to complete the dialogue.

Dad Hi, Nina. How was the school trip?
Nina Great! I've ¹ ___ got back.
Dad Mum's ² ___ to the Chinese takeaway. She's getting chicken fried rice. I hope you're hungry.
Nina Not really. I've ³ ___ eaten. I had a burger about two hours ago.
Dad Oh. I'll ring mum. Perhaps she hasn't bought the food ⁴ ___. Where's my phone? I'll go and look in my bedroom.
Mum Hello!
Nina Hi, Mum. Dad! Dad! Don't worry about your phone! Mum's ⁵ ___ bought the food. She's ⁶ ___ walked through the front door.
Dad Ah, the smell of Chinese food has made me hungry again!

1 a yet   **b** already   **c** just
2 a gone   **b** went   **c** been
3 a already **b** yet   **c** just
4 a already **b** just   **c** yet
5 a already **b** yet   **c** just
6 a yet   **b** just   **c** already

5 ★★★ USE OF ENGLISH Complete the texts with one word in each gap.

Hi Tim,
I'm having problems with my Maths homework. My sister's ¹*gone* out so I can't ask her to help me. Have you done the homework ² _____?
Kirsten

Hi Kirsten,
Sorry I didn't answer your text earlier. I've ³ _____ come back from basketball training. I need a shower! ⁴ _____ you finished the Maths homework yet?

Tim, I still need help, please!

Kirsten, you're right. It is difficult! My brother ⁵ _____ just told me about a great YouTube channel with very helpful Maths videos. I'll send you the link and I'm sure you'll do the homework!

6 ON A HIGH NOTE Write about some things which have already happened, just happened or haven't happened yet in your life.

115

10D READING AND VOCABULARY

1 Read the text quickly and match the numbers from the box with what they refer to.

2000	5000	80 percent	12 percent	38 million	½

1 The number of tourists to Thailand each year. _38 million_

2 The amount of damaged or destroyed coral at Maya Bay. _____

3 The first year when you could see *The Beach* in cinemas. _____

4 The number of centimetres coral grows every year. _____

5 The daily number of visitors to Maya Bay. _____

6 This is how much money the tourism industry produces in Thailand. _____

2 Read the text again and choose the correct answers.

1 According to the text, what happened because of the film *The Beach*?

  a 2000 people come to Maya Bay every day.

  b It made Maya Bay more popular.

  c The main actor became a star.

  d The Thai government built roads to the beach.

2 Which of the reasons does the text NOT mention as a cause of damage to the coral reef?

  a boats

  b swimmers

  c rubbish

  d sun cream

3 What caused problems to wildlife near Maya Bay?

  a parties at night

  b no toilets on the beach

  c rubbish on the beach

  d people exploring the island

4 What did the Thai government decide in June 2018?

  a To close the beach until the coral recovers.

  b To introduce fees for visitors to Maya Bay.

  c To keep the beach open until the main tourist season.

  d To close the beach for a short time.

5 What is the writer's view of the ban?

  a It will reduce the number of tourists to Thailand.

  b It will lead to similar problems in other places.

  c The coral will recover very quickly.

  d It will make people care more for the environment.

6 What would be a good title for the article?

  a Film shows problems of mass tourism.

  b Tourists are becoming more environmentally friendly.

  c Thai government finally tries to save popular beach.

  d Visit Maya Bay before it becomes too popular.

Vocabulary extension

3 Match the highlighted words from the text with the definitions.

1 Continue, to stay the same. _remain_

2 Get better and return to normal. _____

3 Made someone decide to do something by telling them why it's a good idea. _____

4 Had a bad effect on something. _____

5 Ruined something so badly you can't use or repair it. _____

4 Complete the sentences with the correct forms of the verbs from Exercise 3.

1 The storm _damaged_ our house. It broke two windows and some of the roof fell off.

2 Let's try to _____ Agnes to come to our party.

3 When my dad went back to the town he grew up in, it was completely different. Only about two buildings _____ from when he was a boy.

4 I'm sorry you feel ill. I hope you _____ soon.

5 The storm _____ our caravan. There are just a few pieces of wood, glass and plastic left on the ground.

ACTIVE VOCABULARY | Suffix *-ful*

One way of forming adjectives from nouns is to add the suffix *-ful*. Sometimes, we have to change the spelling of the noun (e.g. *beauty – beautiful*).

5 Complete the sentences below with the correct adjectives formed from the nouns in the box.

beauty	care	colour	success	use	wonder

1 Vietnam is a very _beautiful_ country with forests, mountains and sandy beaches.

2 I'm having a really _____ time on holiday.

3 I went diving last week and saw a _____ fish. It was blue, pink, yellow and purple.

4 You have to be _____ when you go on a jungle walk as there may be snakes in the grass.

5 Thanks a lot for the guidebook. It was really _____. It's got lots of information that has helped me.

6 It's great news about your blog. I really hope it is _____ and becomes popular.

6 ON A HIGH NOTE Write about a place in your country which has problems because of the number of tourists and a place which is still beautiful and quiet.

UNIT VOCABULARY PRACTICE > page 121

In 2000, Leonardo di Caprio, already a huge star, played the main part in the adventure film *The Beach* about a young traveller in Thailand. The beach in the film, Maya Bay on one of Thailand's tropical islands, wasn't very famous at the time. The only way to get to it is by sea so most tourists didn't know about it.

The film was very successful and soon the beach became a huge tourist attraction. Thousands of people wanted to see this beautiful place. Tourists travelled by road to the nearest town and, from there, motorboats transported up to 5000 people a day to the beach. Unfortunately, boats damaged the coral reef when they came into the bay. People also damaged the reef because they often stood on it while swimming. Another problem was pollution from sun cream which washed into the sea as people swam. In fact, these things together destroyed or damaged about 80 percent of the coral. On land, there was less damage. Most people stayed on the beach and didn't explore the island. On the beach, though, there were only a few bins and toilets. Not enough for 5000 people. Some companies even started organising camping on the beach at night. The loud music and bright lights caused more problems for wildlife on the island.

Because tourism is important for the Thai economy, the government didn't want to close the beach. 12 percent of Thailand's money comes from tourism and there are about 38 million visitors a year. Visitors to Maya Bay have to pay to go there and the money helps the government a lot. However, in June 2018, the government decided to do something to help the coral recover. June is not a busy time for tourists because it rains a lot. At first the government decided to close the beach for four months starting in June. It could open again in time for the main tourist season from November to February. However, in October, an environmental campaign persuaded the government to keep the beach closed until the coral recovers. Coral grows by about ½ a centimetre a year, so it could stay closed for a very long time.

It's great news for Maya Bay but tourist numbers remain high. Now that Maya Bay is closed, other beaches will become more crowded. People will still be more interested in their own enjoyment than the environment, so these beaches will suffer from the same sort of environmental problems.

10E LISTENING AND VOCABULARY

1 🔊 **72 Listen to four conversations and number descriptions a–d below.**

a ☐ A weather forecast.

b ☑ A conversation about different ways of forecasting the weather.

c ☐ A conversation about weather in a different country.

d ☐ A podcast about differences in weather forecasts.

2 🔊 **72 Listen to the conversations again and choose the correct answers.**

1 Which animals can help you to guess what the weather will be like even when you can't see them?

   a birds

   b frogs

   c cats

2 What do you learn about online weather forecasts?

   a They get different information about the weather.

   b They are rarely correct.

   c They can't predict the weather for more than a few days in advance.

3 What does the girl say about Egypt?

   a The summers were too hot for her.

   b She misses the weather there.

   c There are fewer seasons there.

4 What do we know about the temperature in New South Wales?

   a Records show that the highest temperature there was in 1939.

   b The hottest temperature ever there was 48.2˚C.

   c The hot weather will continue for the rest of the week.

Vocabulary extension

3 🔊 **73 Complete the sentences with the words from the box, which you heard in the recording in Exercise 1. Listen and check.**

blow   dry   extreme   heatwave   leaves   ~~satellites~~

1 Different weather websites and apps all use information from *satellites*.

2 We can't be sure of future weather because we can't be sure which way the wind will _____.

3 It's very _____ this summer. We haven't had any rain for two months.

4 _____ weather is when it's much hotter, windier, wetter or colder than normal.

5 Autumn colours are red, brown and yellow. That's the colour of the _____ on the trees at that time of year.

6 We had a _____ for ten days and temperatures were over 40˚C every day.

4 ON A HIGH NOTE **Write a short paragraph saying which is your favourite season of the year and why.**

Pronunciation

ACTIVE PRONUNCIATION | /ɔɪ/ sound

In some words you can hear two different vowel sounds in one syllable (e.g toy /ɔɪ/).
We can spell /ɔɪ/ as oy in **toy** or oi in **voi**ce.

5 🔊 **74 Look at the sentences from the recording in Exercise 1. Which word in each sentence has the /ɔɪ/ sound? Listen, check and repeat.**

1 When rain is coming, they make more noise.

2 I enjoyed the long, hot, dry summers.

6 🔊 **75 Listen to seven words and write them correctly.**

1 *join*   **5** _____

2 _____   **6** _____

3 _____   **7** _____

4 _____

7 🔊 **76 Complete the words with *oi* or *oy*. Listen, check and repeat.**

1 v*oi*ce

2 p__ __nt

3 b__ __l

4 b__ __

5 t__ __

6 n__ __se

8 🔊 **77 Complete the text with the correct words from Exercise 6. Listen and check.**

This girl and ¹*boy* don't want people to ²_____ the planet. They want people to ³_____ their campaign to find clean energy instead of ⁴_____ and gas.

UNIT VOCABULARY PRACTICE > page 121

10F SPEAKING

1 🔊 *78* **Listen and repeat the phrases. How do you say them in your language?**

SPEAKING | Giving and reacting to personal news

GIVING GOOD NEWS

Good news!

I've got some good/fantastic/great news.

I've just heard the results of the Go Green! competition.

GIVING BAD NEWS

I'm afraid I've got some bad/terrible/awful news.

I'm sorry, but I've got some bad news.

Unfortunately, I've got bad news for you.

RESPONDING TO GOOD NEWS

Oh, wow!

Well done!

Good for you!

That's great/amazing news.

Congratulations!

I'm really happy for you.

RESPONDING TO BAD NEWS

Oh, no!

Never mind.

That's terrible/awful news.

Bad luck!

Don't worry.

---

2 **Choose the correct words to complete the sentences.**

1 Good *news / luck*. We came first in the competition.

2 I'm afraid I've got some *terrible / fantastic* news.

3 Oh, *no / wow*! That's amazing!

4 *Good / Well* for you.

5 Never *worry / mind*.

6 I'm really *lucky / happy* for you.

7 Don't *worry / mind*.

3 **Match the two parts of the sentences.**

1 ☐ Bad   **a** done!

2 ☐ I'm sorry,   **b** terrible.

3 ☐ Unfortunately,   **c** news! We've won the match!

4 ☐ I've just   **d** luck!

5 ☐ Well   **e** no!

6 ☐ That's   **f** I've got some bad news.

7 ☐ Oh,   **g** but I've got some bad news.

8 ☐ Good   **h** heard about your excellent exam results.

4 **Choose two correct options to complete the mini-conversation.**

Jane I've got some bad news. Mum's ill and I can't have the party this weekend.

Lucy ¹__

a Never mind.

b Good for you.

c Bad luck.

Sam Great news! I've passed my driving test.

Rob ²__

a Congratulations!

b Don't worry.

c Well done.

Kerry We've won 1st prize in the competition!

Paul ³__

a Wow!

b That's amazing!

c That's terrible.

Kate ⁴__

Mark Oh, no!

a Unfortunately, it's raining.

b I've lost my phone.

c Fantastic news.

Megan ⁵__

Arthur Good for you!

a I've got some terrible news.

b I've found a new job.

c I came top of the class in Maths.

5 🔊 *79* **Complete the mini-conversations with one word in each gap. Listen and check.**

Amber I've got some bad news. We've got a test this afternoon.

Jade Oh, ¹*no*! I haven't done any work for it.

Amber Don't ²_____. No one has! It's a surprise test.

Lionel Fantastic news! I'm in the school football team.

Cristiano Well ³_____. I'm really ⁴_____ for you.

Courtney The weather forecast for Saturday is for rain.

Sophie Never ⁵_____. We can watch a film at home.

Rob Mum, I got 94 percent in my English test.

Mum Oh, ⁶_____. That's great. ⁷_____ for you.

Rob Unfortunately, I only got 65 percent in Maths.

10G WRITING | An article

What a waste!

I live in a large town with a lot of shops and businesses in the centre. Sometimes, when I go out with my friends in the evening, we look in the shop windows and talk about what we'd like to buy. However, a few weeks ago, we had a lesson about energy and discussed why we should turn off lights, television sets and other things when we aren't using them. Producing energy causes pollution because we still get most of our electricity from coal, gas and oil.

Now when I walk in the town centre after dark I don't think about the clothes and gadgets in the shop windows. I think about the huge amount of electricity that the businesses are wasting. There are lights on in all the shops and most of the offices. In the electrical shop, there are about twenty television sets which stay on all night. It's terrible.

I think we should have a campaign to make businesses switch all the lights off when they are closed. I've talked to my teacher about it and she thinks it's a great idea. She's going to help us to organise a petition in our next lesson about the environment.

In my opinion, businesses and individuals use much more electricity than they need to and we have to tell them why it's so dangerous for our planet.

- Add an interesting title.
- Introduce the topic.
- Give examples of the problem.
- Give examples of what you can do about the problem.
- Add a short conclusion and finish with an interesting sentence.

1 Read the article and tick the petition that best matches its content.

1 ☐ Save electricity!

We want shops and offices to close earlier so that they don't need to keep their lights on for so long each day.

Sign our petition!

2 ☐ Stop wasting energy!

Join our campaign to force shops and businesses to use more clean energy. Gas, coal and oil cause pollution. Wind, sun and water don't!

Sign our petition now!

3 ☐ Don't waste electricity!

Why do businesses keep their lights on when no one is working? We want to force businesses to switch off at the end of the working day.

Please sign our petition.

2 Match problems 1–6 with possible article titles a–f.

1 ☐ noise pollution – from traffic, machines or noisy neighbours

2 ☐ light pollution – bright lights that make it difficult to sleep

3 ☐ animals – dogs and cats which don't have homes

4 ☐ litter – in the street

5 ☐ traffic problems – too many people driving to and from work

6 ☐ air pollution – from traffic, factories, fires

a It's quicker to walk.
b I can't breathe!
c Put it in the bin.
d Please be quiet!
e The homeless aren't all human.
f Blinded by the light.

3 WRITING TASK Read the advert and write an article about one of the problems in Exercise 2.

Articles wanted!

What problem do you have in your local area?

Why is it a problem?

What can people do about the problem?

Write an article. Answer these questions and we will publish the most interesting articles in our magazine.

ACTIVE WRITING | An article

1 Plan your article.
- Use one of the ideas from Exercise 2 for your problem.
- Try to think of a better title than the idea in Exercise 2.
- List vocabulary you could use in your article.

2 Write the article.
- Write an interesting title.
- Start by explaining the problem.
- Answer the questions in the task.
- Use adjectives and adverbs to make your writing more interesting.
- Use paragraphs to make your article easy to read.

3 Check that ...
- you have included all the relevant information.
- there are no spelling or grammar mistakes.

UNIT VOCABULARY PRACTICE

1 10A GRAMMAR AND VOCABULARY **Complete the words in the sentences with one letter in each gap.**

1 This is a great place for families. Warm sea and the best b _e_ _a_ _c_ h on this part of the c __ __ __ t. The water is clean, and the kids love playing in the lovely yellow s __ __ d.

2 We can swim to the i __ __ __ __ d in the middle of the l __ __ e.

3 You can't go kayaking on this r __ __ __ r. There are lots of dangerous r __ __ __ s under the water and then a 15-metre high w __ __ __ __ __ f __ __ l.

4 I like walking along this v __ __ __ __ y between the m __ __ __ t __ __ __ s. Actually, they're only about 700 metres high so maybe I should say 'between the h __ __ __ s'.

5 The Baltic is a s __ __ but the Atlantic is an o __ __ __ n.

6 There are huge areas of trees in Russia and Brazil but there is one big difference. In Russia, there are f __ __ __ __ __ s but in Brazil there's a big j __ __ __ __ e.

7 There are no flowers or trees here. There are no plants because there is no water. It's a d __ __ __ __ t.

2 10B VOCABULARY **Label the pictures.**

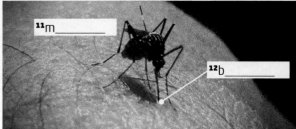

1 d_uck_
2 w_____
3 b_____
4 f_____
5 c_____
6 s_____
7 t_____
8 m_____
9 f_____
10 t_____
11 m_____
12 b_____

3 10D READING AND VOCABULARY **Complete the dialogues with the words from the box.**

ban campaign ~~petition~~ pollution research wildlife

David Could you sign my **1**_petition_, please?
Man What's it for?
David We're organising a **2**_____ about the traffic problems in this town. We want to **3**_____ cars from the town centre.
Man That's where I work. I need my car. I'm not signing this.

Mum Did you have an interesting day at school?
Ben Yes, we learned that scientists in our local area are doing lots of **4**_____ about all the problems that **5**_____ from traffic and factories causes.
Mum Like what?
Ben Well, for example, it's bad for animals. Well, all **6**_____ – animals, birds, insects and fish. The water is dirty, they can't breathe and there is less food for them to eat.

4 10E LISTENING AND VOCABULARY **Complete the mini-conversations with the words in bold and adjectives formed from them.**

1 CLOUD
Kelly It's very _cloudy_ today.
Sandra Yes, that big grey _cloud_ over there doesn't look nice at all.

2 FOG
Ahmed I can't see anything because of the _____.
Phil I know. It's really _____ today.

3 SUN
Anna What a lovely _____ day!
Lucy Be careful! The _____ is very strong. Put a hat on.

4 WIND
Mick Is it often _____ here?
Gerry Yes, but the _____ comes from the south so it's usually warm.

5 RAIN
Molly When will this _____ stop?
Pam Not today. The forecast says it will be _____ all day.

6 STORM
Noah Did you hear that? I think a _____ is coming.
Mark I don't think so. It isn't a _____ day.

7 SNOW
Sonia I'd like to live in a _____ country like Canada.
Suzie Yes, not going to school because the _____ is 2 metres deep.

5 ON A HIGH NOTE **What activities do you do in different kinds of weather?**

1 **For each learning objective, write 1–5 to assess your ability.**

1 = I don't feel confident. 5 = I feel confident.

	Learning objective	Course material	How confident I am (1–5)
10A	I can use the Present Perfect to talk about experiences.	Student's Book pp. 128–129 Workbook pp. 112–113	
10B	I can talk about animals.	Student's Book p. 130 Workbook p. 114	
10C	I can use the Present Perfect to talk about past events that are important now.	Student's Book p. 131 Workbook p. 115	
10D	I can understand specific information in a longer text and talk about the environment.	Student's Book pp. 132–133 Workbook pp. 116–117	
10E	I can understand the context and identify specific information in a conversation and talk about weather.	Student's Book p. 134 Workbook p. 118	
10F	I can give and react to good and bad news.	Student's Book p. 135 Workbook p. 119	
10G	I can write an article.	Student's Book p. 136 Workbook p. 120	

2 **Which of the skills above would you like to improve in? How?**

Skill I want to improve in	How I can improve

3 **What can you remember from this unit?**

New words I learned and most want to remember	Expressions and phrases I liked	English I heard or read outside class

GRAMMAR AND VOCABULARY

1 Choose the correct words a–c to complete the sentences.

1 Ow! This bird has got a really sharp ___.
a feather   b tail   c beak

2 I can hear a ___. I hope it doesn't come and drink my blood!
a bee   b mosquito   c fly

3 A lot of the land is ___. There's no rain and nothing grows there.
a jungle   b valley   c desert

4 That monkey has got a really long ___.
a beak   b wing   c tail

5 I like to go on holiday by the ___ because I like swimming in the sea.
a coast   b forest   c sand

/ 5

2 Match the words from the box with their definitions.

ant   feathers   fur   island   ~~lake~~   whale

1 It's an area of water. *lake*
2 It lives in the sea and can be bigger than an elephant. _____
3 Birds have these all over their body. _____
4 It's land in the middle of water. _____
5 It's a small insect. _____
6 It's the hair of some animals. _____

/ 5

3 Complete the text with the words from the box. There is one extra word.

already   ~~ever~~   has   have   just   never   yet

HAVE YOU ¹*EVER* THOUGHT
OF BECOMING A VOLUNTEER?

Kylie is only 17 but she has ²_____ helped on three projects. On these projects, she ³_____ taught English to people from other countries, looked after wildlife in Scotland and helped on a green farm. In fact, she has ⁴_____ returned from the farm and hasn't even had time to change her clothes ⁵_____.

Kylie works very hard and doesn't have time for summer holidays, but she has ⁶_____ felt upset when her friends have told her about their relaxing holidays in the sun.

/ 5

4 Use the prompts to make questions and answers in the Present Perfect.

Sven   you / ever / be / to Iceland?
¹*Have you ever been to Iceland?*

Agatha   no / not
²_____

Jo   Your brother looks upset. What / happen?
³_____

Elaine   He / just / find out / that he's got a test tomorrow.
⁴_____

Darren   your parents / sell / their car yet?
⁵_____

Chris   No. Why? Do you want to buy it?

Darren   No! I / not pass / my test yet.
⁶_____

/ 5

USE OF ENGLISH

5 Complete the second sentence using the word in bold so that it means the same as the first one. Use no more than three words including the word in bold.

1 I'll do my homework later. **DONE**
I *haven't done* my homework yet.

2 We finished this unit in an earlier lesson. **ALREADY**
We _____ this unit.

3 Don't leave the television on when you go to bed. **OFF**
Don't forget to _____ the television when you go to bed.

4 Michael wrote me an email a few seconds ago. **JUST**
Michael _____ me an email.

5 This is my first visit to Italy. **BEEN**
I _____ to Italy before.

6 The wind is very strong today. **VERY**
It _____ today.

/ 5

6 Complete the sentences with the correct words formed from the words in bold.

1 At last, a *sunny* day. Let's go swimming! **SUN**

2 What's the worst _____ problem in your country? **ENVIRONMENT**

3 Come and see the amazing _____, including elephants, tigers and bears. **LIFE**

4 The cars drove slowly because it was a very _____ morning. **FOG**

5 The _____ in the centre of town is terrible because of all the cars. **POLLUTE**

6 Niagara Falls aren't the biggest _____ in the world but they could be the most famous. **FALL**

/ 5

/ 30

123

PHRASAL VERBS

be away: My big sister is away at university so I use her bedroom.
be fed up with: Are you fed up with football? Try basketball!
be out: I can only listen to loud music when my parents are out.
check out: Check snow kayaking out. It's so cool!
clean up: It took two weeks to clean up the farm!
clear away: Clear your rubbish away if you have a barbecue on the beach.
come along: We're going to the cinema. Why don't you come along?
come back: What does Jasper do when Joy comes back home?
come from: Our teacher comes from London in England.
come on: Come on, let's go and buy some ice cream!
come out: *Brothers* is a comedy film. It came out over five years ago.
come over: At weekends my friends come over and we listen to music.
eat in: Why do people often eat in at home these days?
eat out: Why don't we eat out in this new restaurant tonight?
fall over: Be careful! The wind is so strong I almost fell over.
find out: To find out more about these courses, visit our website.
get around: How does she plan to get around Oxford?
get back: When you go out, do you ever get back after midnight?
get on/off: Inform the driver when you want to get on or off the bus.
get up: I get up at 6 a.m. every day.
give out: At Harriet's, staff give out free coffee in the morning.
give up: Don't give up so easily. I'm sure you can do this exercise.
go away: I go away on holiday with my family twice a year.
go back: You can go back to Manchester by coach.
go on: Go on! Do it! Don't be afraid.
go out with sb: On Saturdays I go out with friends.
go with: Those running shoes don't go with that smart dress.
grow up: As she grows up she becomes more confident.
hang out: On Saturdays I hang out with my friends.
heat up: Dinner is in the oven. Just heat it up for ten minutes.
help out: Do you sometimes help your mum out at home?
hold on: Hold on a minute. I need to wash my hands first.
hurry up: Hurry up! The bus leaves in ten minutes.
look after: Who looks after Jasper when the family is away?
look for: Snakes come out at night to look for food.
look forward to: I'm looking forward to mountain biking tomorrow.
look up: We look up information about important events online.
miss out: Don't miss out because our baker makes excellent cakes!
pick up: A bird uses its beak to pick up and eat food.
pick up: I can pick you up in the car today.
point sth out: She pointed out that only Jane knew the answer.
put away: You must put everything away at the end of the lesson.
put down: Put down your pens when you finish the exam.
put on: My parents often put on their favourite songs in the car.
put on: I didn't remember to put sun cream on and I got sunburnt!
sell out: Even at this price, the tickets usually sell out in a few hours.
show up: 1,500 people showed up for two days of rock and folk music.
slow down: He doesn't stop for lunch because it slows him down!
start up: My computer wasn't cheap but it starts up really slowly.
stay in: Some teenagers stay in all the time and play computer games.
stay up: I often stay up till 2 a.m. It's quieter and I can study.
switch off: Do you ever switch your phone off?
switch on: My phone isn't working. It doesn't even switch on.
take out: I often take our neighbours' dog out in the afternoon.
take out: Take your phone out and start the app.
throw away: I never throw away good food.
try on: Can I try these jeans on?
try out: Can I try this smart fork out?
turn down: We need to turn the music down because it's too noisy.
turn off: Turn off the notifications on your phone.
turn on: It's dark. Turn the lights on.
turn up: Turn up the speakers. I can't hear the music.
wake up: My bed is under the window, so it's very light when I wake up.
warm up: You should always warm up before you do a sport.
wash up: You can wash up the dishes or make food.
work out: They work out in the gym for an hour.

PREPOSITIONS

PREPOSITIONS IN PHRASES

AT
at (eight) o'clock: She usually eats dinner at eight o'clock.
at first: The tracker beeps quietly at first and then it starts beeping loudly.
at home: We don't live near a cinema so I watch films at home.
at lunchtime: What kind of food can you have there at lunchtime?
at midnight: There's a great film on TV at midnight.
at night: Don't revise late at night! You should go to bed early.
at school: At school, we also talk about important events or problems.
at the café/restaurant: Robin is at the café and is eating a chocolate cake.
at the centre of: The audience feel that they're at the centre of the action.
at the cinema: I quite like watching films at the cinema.
at the moment: Are you learning anything new at the moment?
at the seaside: Anna is going to spend the weekend at the seaside.
at weekends: At JBJ you can only eat at weekends.

BY
by bus/car/plane/train: Do you get to school by car or by bus?
by (ten) o'clock: John has no breakfast and he's hungry by ten o'clock.

FOR
for breakfast: What do you usually have for breakfast?
for free: He works for free in the kitchen.
for example/instance: For instance, there are already 'smart' lights and fridges.
for rent: Is there a flat or house for rent?

FROM
from Monday to Sunday: You can visit the café from Monday to Sunday.

IN
in August/May/etc.: Jane usually goes on holiday in August.
in bed: It's really quiet and so I just stay in bed.
in your free time: In my free time I like playing computer games.
in your opinion: In my opinion, there are four key stages in a project.
in the future: We'll use these gadgets a lot in the future.
in the middle of: It's on a river in the middle of a jungle!
in the morning/afternoon/evening: My favourite dish is only available in the morning.
in the mountains: These students are from a tiny village in the mountains.
in the park: We sometimes play football in the park after school.
in the past: In History we study important events in the past.
in the photo: There's a beautiful blue background in this photo.
in the summer: We're going to have a barbecue sometime in the summer.

ON
on a farm: It started on a farm in 1970, the day after Jimi Hendrix died.
on an island: At the end of the film, Pi frees the tiger on a deserted island.
on Earth: It's the largest building on Earth; you can see it from space.
on foot: My dad gets to work on foot.
on Friday/Monday/etc: The weekend starts on Friday in the UAE.
on holiday: I'm not going shopping when I'm on holiday in New York!
on the bus/train/plane/etc.: I sometimes read a newspaper on the bus.
on the Internet: There's a lot of useful information on the Internet.
on the left/right: Go past the museum and the park is on the left.
on the menu: On the cat theme menu there are some speciality drinks.
on the news: I heard about the accident on the news.
on the phone: They're always on their phones.
on the website: That's it, Amber. The flat's on the website.
on time: Phil isn't going to get to the cinema on time.
on TV: Millions of people watched the wedding of Diana and Charles on TV.
on Wednesday afternoon: I'm going shopping on Wednesday afternoon.
on weekdays: Anna goes to bed at ten o'clock on weekdays.

PREPOSITIONS AFTER NOUNS

advice for: Do you have any advice for young directors?

advice on: In pairs, ask for and give advice on which sports you should do.

argument with: I feel stressed when I have an argument with my friend.

campaign against: They started a campaign against plastic bags.

congratulations on: Congratulations on winning the first place in the race!

conversation about: We often have a conversation about the weather.

conversation with: He dreams of having a conversation with his robot.

experience of: Teenagers don't have the experience of adults.

experience with: What was Thomas's first experience with graffiti?

expert in: Today our guest is Claire Price, an expert in the history of clothes.

expert on: He's a radio interviewer and an expert on street art.

film about: A documentary is a film about real people and events.

grade in: I got good grades in all my subjects at school this year.

guide to: A brief guide to the UK's number 1 music and arts festival.

ideas on: Could you share your ideas on how to revise before exams?

lesson about: I enjoyed our school lesson about world leaders.

opinion about: What's your opinion about this school?

passion for: We're looking for artists with a passion for the environment.

present for: How often do you buy presents for your friends?

presentation about: What was your History presentation about?

project on: The whole school is doing a project on nature this term.

qualification in: They also get a qualification in designing computer games.

reason for: What is the most important reason for giving storms names?

rules of: Do you have to know the rules of hockey?

taste in: What do we know about Oliver's taste in music?

time for: It's time for bed. It's already ten p.m.

work on: It's important to plan your work on the project together.

PREPOSITIONS AFTER ADJECTIVES

afraid of: My mum's afraid of nothing. She is very brave.

allergic to: I'm allergic to nuts.

angry with: Dad never gets angry with us – he's great!

dangerous to: Which animals are the most dangerous to humans?

different from: Oliver's taste in music is very different from his brother's.

excited about: I was excited about this film but it was really disappointing.

famous for: What would you like to be famous for?

good at: My favourite club is Spanish but I'm not very good at it.

good for: Eating too many cakes isn't good for you.

happy for: What a wonderful opportunity! I'm so happy for you.

important to: Tourism is important to the island.

interested in: They are hardly ever interested in the real world.

late for: It's a good idea to leave home early so you aren't late for school.

nervous about: Are you nervous about travelling alone?

patient with: She was always very patient with me.

ready for: But are we ready for a robot like Pepper in our daily lives?

similar to: You can be a lookalike if you look similar to a famous person.

stressed about: I'm stressed about my exams.

successful in: Was Cassie successful in her interview?

surprised about: The girl felt surprised about the quality of the picture.

terrible at: No, sorry – I'm terrible at Maths!

worried about: I'm really worried about the Maths exam tomorrow.

PREPOSITIONS AFTER VERBS

agree with: My sister doesn't agree with me. We argue quite often.

appear in: Five best posters will also appear in their campaign.

arrive at: It's 8.45 a.m. and some students are arriving at school.

ask for: Ask your teacher for help.

attach to: Attach a USB cable to your phone.

believe in: I don't believe in myself. I'm not confident.

care about: Emily thinks that teenagers care about the real world.

chat with: We usually have a snack and chat with friends.

choose from: There are 30 vegetarian dishes – too many to choose from!

concentrate on: You should concentrate on your work better.

decide on: Talk to your friend and decide on the best place to go.

depend on: My results depend on how many kilometres I cycle every day.

divide by: When you divide one hundred by four, you get twenty-five.

dream about: I look at the pictures and dream about the homes.

dream of: I'm actually dreaming of taking part in a triathlon.

experiment with: I think scientists will continue to experiment with that machine.

feel about: How did Thomas feel about art classes at school?

focus on: Do you always focus very well on your homework?

get to: How do you usually get to school?

laugh at: I never read them with friends. They laugh at me!

learn about: Can you learn about vegetarianism at Indian Veg?

listen to: They always listen to terrible music.

look at: I love eating food and I also love looking at it.

pay for: At JBJ you never pay for a meal.

prefer sth to sth: Teenagers prefer talking about news to reading news.

prepare for: What does Alistair do to prepare for triathlons?

protect from: Space suits protect your skin from radiation.

rely on: This film doesn't rely on amazing special effects to tell the story.

revise for: I find revising for exams really stressful.

share with: Don't share your passwords with anyone.

shout at: Calm down and stop shouting at me.

speak to: Why should Cassie speak to Simon?

spend on: Jonathan Davey spends £10,000 on flights every year.

stay with: I'm studying English in Oxford and staying with a host family.

suffer from: We suffer from many environmental problems in this area.

take care of: Take care of yourself: try to get eight hours sleep every night.

take part in: Our students can take part in a school exchange project.

talk about: At school, we also talk about important events or problems.

talk to: I'm going to talk to the class about my predictions for the future.

tell about: I never tell anyone about my extra sleep.

think of: Can you think of the advantages of walking to school?

travel around: We are going to travel around Europe this summer.

travel from: Did you travel from Oslo to Stockholm by train?

travel to: How do you travel to school?

volunteer for: Which project does Cassie want to volunteer for?

wait for: I wait for my parents to go to work.

waste sth on: Her parents sometimes waste time on their phones.

work as: Tom went to South Africa to work as a volunteer.

work at: Over 1,500 people volunteer to work at Glastonbury.

work for: Sam works for a company called Citysprint.

work with: What food is difficult to work with?

worry about: I worry about my bad diet. I eat too much fast food.

write about: A reviewer visits restaurants, tries the food and writes about it.

TIMES AND DATES

DAYS OF THE WEEK
Monday
Tuesday
Wednesday
Thursday
Friday
Saturday
Sunday

MONTHS

January	July
February	August
March	September
April	October
May	November
June	December

CARDINAL NUMBERS

1 – one	17 – seventeen
2 – two	18 – eighteen
3 – three	19 – nineteen
4 – four	20 – twenty
5 – five	21 – twenty-one
6 – six	22 – twenty-two
7 – seven	23 – twenty-three
8 – eight	30 – thirty
9 – nine	40 – forty
10 – ten	50 – fifty
11 – eleven	60 – sixty
12 – twelve	70 – seventy
13 – thirteen	80 – eighty
14 – fourteen	90 – ninety
15 – fifteen	100 – one hundred
16 – sixteen	

ORDINAL NUMBERS

1st – first	17th – seventeenth
2nd – second	18th – eighteenth
3rd – third	19th – nineteenth
4th – fourth	20th – twentieth
5th – fifth	21st – twenty-first
6th – sixth	22nd – twenty-second
7th – seventh	23rd – twenty-third
8th – eighth	30th – thirtieth
9th – ninth	40th – fortieth
10th – tenth	50th – fiftieth
11th – eleventh	60th – sixtieth
12th – twelfth	70th – seventieth
13th – thirteenth	80th – eightieth
14th – fourteenth	90th – ninetieth
15th – fifteenth	100th –hundredth
16th – sixteenth	101st – hundred and first

31/3/1992: The thirty-first of March, nineteen ninety-two.
12/11/2020: The twelfth of November, twenty twenty
5/2/2004: The fifth of February, two thousand and four.
9/6/1778: The ninth of June, seventeen seventy-eight.
24th July: The twenty-fourth of July.
13th July: The thirteenth of July.
22nd April: The twenty-second of April.

TELLING THE TIME
6.00: It's six o'clock.
3.15: It's quarter past three.
2.30: It's half past two.
3.45: It's quarter to four.
12.50: It's ten to one.
24.00: It's midnight.

WORD BUILDING

PREFIXES THAT GIVE AN OPPOSITE MEANING

Prefix	Examples
un-	uncomfortable, unusual
im-	impossible, impatient
dis-	disagree, discover

SUFFIXES

Noun suffixes

Suffix	Examples
-er	photographer, reviewer
-or	actor, sculptor
-ist	scientist, tourist
-ian	musician, dietician
-ment	equipment, announcement
-ion	pollution, suggestion
-ness	fitness, illness

Adjective suffixes

Suffix	Examples
-y	windy, snowy
-ous	dangerous, famous
-ed	amazed, excited
-lng	exciting, disappointing

Adverb suffixes

Suffix	Examples
-ly	loudly, easily

Verb suffixes

Suffix	Examples
-ate	create, nominate
-ise/-ize	advise, summarize
-ify	justify, modify

PRONUNCIATION TABLE

Consonants

p   perfect, helpful, happen
b   bossy, hobby, job
t   tennis, actor, attend
d   degree, middle, word
k   kiss, school, ask, coach
g   get, luggage, ghost
tʃ check, match, future
dʒ bridge, page, soldier
f   false, difficult, laugh, physical
v   verb, nervous, move
θ   third, author, bath
ð   this, father, with
s   saw, notice, sister
z   zone, amazing, choose, quiz
ʃ   ship, sure, station, ocean
ʒ   pleasure, occasion
h   had, whole, chocoholic
m   melon, common, sum
n   neat, know, channel, sun
ŋ   cooking, long, thanks, sung
l   lifestyle, magically, kettle
r   respect, correct, arrival
j   year, use, beautiful
w   window, one, where

Vowels

ɪ   gift, invite
e   gentle, bed
æ   bad, matchbox, plan
ɒ   lot, optimistic, wash
ʌ   love, but, luck
ʊ   foot, good, put
iː reading, three, magazine
eɪ race, pay, break
aɪ twice, bright, try
ɔɪ enjoy, disappointed
uː two, blue, school
əʊ boat, below, no
aʊ shout, now
ɪə year, here, serious
eə chair, various, square
ɑː mark, father
ɔː bought, draw, author
ʊə tourist, flower
ɜː hurt, third
i   happy, pronunciation, serious
ə   apprentice, actor
u   situation, visual, influence

SELF-CHECK ANSWER KEY

Unit 1
Exercise 1
1a 2c 3b 4c 5b
Exercise 2
1 at 2 put 3 in 4 about 5 up 6 have
Exercise 3
1 My friends never play chess after school.
2 Are you often late for your lessons?
3 I don't often watch reality TV.
4 I like listening to all kinds of music.
5 I think watching television is a waste of time.
6 I have guitar lessons twice a week.
Exercise 4
1 Do you wear 2 often sings 3 Does your mum like 4 doesn't read 5 does Ellie check 6 are always
Exercise 5
1 do 2 front 3 Does 4 have 5 week 6 times (days)
Exercise 6
1 out until 2 agree with 3 at the weekend 4 can't stand 5 you live in 6 hardly ever write

Unit 2
Exercise 1
1 shelf 2 attic 3 wardrobe 4 sofa 5 washing machine
Exercise 2
1g 2f 3a 4b 5e
Exercise 3
1 How many people are there in your class?
2 There aren't any books in our living room.
3 Can you draw pictures of animals?
4 My teachers can't read my writing.
5 Are there any windows in the cellar?
6 My dad can cook Italian food.
Exercise 4
1 Yes, there is. 2 No, they can't. 3 No, she can't. 4 No, there aren't. 5 Yes, I can. 6 Yes, there is.
Exercise 5
1a 2c 3d 4a 5c
Exercise 6
1 dining 2 messy 3 comfortable 4 traditional 5 information 6 suggestions

Unit 3
Exercise 1
1c 2a 3c 4c 5a
Exercise 2
1e 2c 3b 4d 5a
Exercise 3
1 much 2 any 3 lot 4 too 5 few 6 some
Exercise 4
1c 2c 3b 4c 5a
Exercise 5
1 out 2 of 3 some 4 out 5 as 6 no
Exercise 6
1 speciality 2 starter 3 vegetarians 4 hungry 5 dietician 6 photographers

Unit 4
Exercise 1
1b 2b 3c 4b 5b
Exercise 2
1 freezing 2 dangerous 3 qualifications 4 calculator 5 Education 6 playing
Exercise 3
1a What do you usually do in your free time?
b What are you doing at the moment?
2a Who does Lisa usually sit next to in Maths?
b Who is she sitting next to today?
3a What is your teacher wearing today?
b Does she always wear the same clothes?
Exercise 4
1 are learning 2 happens 3 is staying 4 don't speak 5 speaks 6 is getting
Exercise 5
1b 2c 3a 4c 5a
Exercise 6
1 for 2 At 3 are 4 it 5 on 6 him

Unit 5
Exercise 1
1 personality 2 creative 3 helpful 4 attractive 5 curly 6 beautiful
Exercise 2
1 looks 2 middle-aged 3 goes 4 gloves 5 trainers 6 fair
Exercise 3
1 was, were 2 Did you enjoy, gave 3 didn't laugh, wasn't 4 went, weren't 5 were, changed 6 Did your girlfriend wear, bought
Exercise 4
1 Where did you buy those shoes?
2 How many languages could your grandfather speak when he was a boy?
3 I didn't like the film we saw last night.
4 When did you start learning the piano?
5 Who was that woman in the classroom?
6 When I was young, I always wanted to be a firefighter.
Exercise 5
1 uncle's eyes are 2 lot in 3 try it 4 bald 5 different from 6 does Ben look
Exercise 6
1a 2c 3c 4b 5b

Unit 6
Exercise 1
1 director 2 communicative 3 documentary 4 actors 5 luxurious 6 predictable
Exercise 2
1 cast 2 audience 3 choreographer 4 soundtrack 5 plot 6 composer
Exercise 3
1 than 2 as 3 the 4 more 5 enough 6 too
Exercise 4
1b 2d 3e 4c 5a
Exercise 5
1 was too short 2 is set in 3 not funny enough 4 as easy to 5 the best kind/type 6 sold out
Exercise 6
1 best 2 creative 3 original 4 paintings 5 sculptor 6 talented

Unit 7
Exercise 1
1 take, trip 2 get, job 3 do, sightseeing 4 have, meal 5 train timetable 6 find accommodation
Exercise 2
1 to 2 by 3 on 4 park 5 off 6 on
Exercise 3
1 What are you going to do 2 I'm not going to do 3 He's going to spend 4 We're going to get 5 Are your parents going to bring 6 Elle is going to cook
Exercise 4
1 I'm going to look for a new dress on Friday.
2 I'm meeting Chloe at 10 a.m.
3 She (Chloe) is going to buy some new shoes.
4 Chloe is going to a party with her boyfriend.
5 My cousins are coming for my dad's birthday.
6 My brother and I are going to make him a cake.
Exercise 5
1b 2b 3c 4b 5a
Exercise 6
1 to go to 2 with a host 3 my/the plane ticket 4 'm going to 5 go by bus 6 going to go

Unit 8
Exercise 1
1a 2b 3b 4c 5a
Exercise 2
1 installed 2 type 3 headphones 4 delete 5 produces 6 drone
Exercise 3
1 What time will you arrive
2 Will you be able to find the house?
3 How long will you be able to stay?
4 How many people will (there) be at the party?
5 Will I know them all?
6 Will there be (any) food at the party?
Exercise 4
1a, untidily 2d, slowly 3f, quietly 4b, fast 5e, quickly 6c, badly
Exercise 5
1 carefully 2 charger 3 wireless 4 well 5 reality 6 happily
Exercise 6
1 will 2 disk 3 able 4 charge 5 cable 6 turn

Unit 9
Exercise 1
1 goal 2 goggles 3 karate 4 racket 5 ache 6 mouth
Exercise 2
1 climbing 2 helmets 3 ankle 4 hurt 5 bones 6 muscles
Exercise 3
1 should have 2 mustn't cycle 3 must leave 4 mustn't swim 5 must walk 6 should go
Exercise 4
1 should 2 have to 3 don't 4 shouldn't 5 mustn't 6 must
Exercise 5
1 mustn't play 2 a stomach ache 3 should go to 4 wear goggles 5 don't have 6 the matter
Exercise 6
1a 2c 3c 4b 5a

Unit 10
Exercise 1
1c 2b 3c 4c 5a
Exercise 2
1 lake 2 whale 3 feathers 4 island 5 ant 6 fur
Exercise 3
1 ever 2 already 3 has 4 just 5 yet 6 never
Exercise 4
1 Have you ever been to Iceland?
2 No, I haven't.
3 What's/has happened?
4 He's/has just found out that he's got a test tomorrow.
5 Have your parents sold their car yet?
6 No! I haven't passed my test yet.
Exercise 5
1 haven't done 2 have already finished 3 turn/switch off 4 has just written 5 have never been/haven't been 6 is/'s very windy
Exercise 6
1 sunny 2 environmental 3 wildlife 4 foggy 5 pollution 6 waterfalls